ART TRAVEL GUIDE

MUST-SEE CONTEMPORARY ART SITES ACROSS THE USA

Connie Terwilliger

Art Travel Guide: Must-see contemporary art sites across the USA
by Connie Terwilliger

©2012 by ArtNetwork
Published by ArtNetwork, 10655 Park Ave Ext, Nevada City, CA 95959
530.478.0920 arttravelguide.info
Cover and interior design by Laura Ottina Davis

Front cover artwork by Niki de Saint Phalle, *Queen Califia's Magical Circle*, Kit Carson Park, Escondido. ©2012 Niki Charitable Art Foundation. All rights reserved / ARS, NY / ADAGP, Paris. Photo ©Philipp Scholz-Rittermann. See page 3 for details.
Back cover artwork by Siberfi, a costume-designer and longtime Burning Man participant from London. Photo by Scott London. Burningman.com See page 36 for details.
Interior artwork: Page 38 Jim Lambie ©2012 Artists Rights Society (ARS), New York / DACS, London; pages 41, 45-46, 51 Andy Warhol ©2012 The Andy Warhol Foundation for the Visual Arts, Inc / Artists Rights Society (ARS), New York; pages 17, 41, 87 Sol LeWitt ©2012 The LeWitt Estate / Artists Rights Society (ARS), New York; pages 80, 93-96 Frank Lloyd Wright ©2012 Frank Lloyd Wright Foundation, Scottsdale, AZ / Artists Rights Society (ARS), New York; page 128, *Sun God*, 1983 by Niki de Saint Phalle, Stuart Collection, UC San Diego ©2012 Niki Charitable Art Foundation, All rights reserved / ARS, NY / ADAGP, Paris.

Publisher's Cataloging-in-Publication Data

Terwilliger, Connie.
    Art travel guide : must-see contemporary art
sites across the USA / Connie Terwilliger.
        p. cm.
    ISBN: 978-0-940899-56-8
    1. Arts, American. 2. Art, Modern—21st
century—Guidebooks . 3. United States—
Description and travel.   I. Title.
N410 .T47 2011
708.13—dc22

Library of Congress Control Number: 2011945712

Disclaimer: While the publisher and author have made every reasonable attempt to obtain accurate information and verify same, occasional address and telephone number changes are inevitable, as well as other discrepancies. We assume no liability for errors or omissions in editorial listings. Should you discover any changes, please e-mail the publisher at info@arttravelguide.info so that corrections may be made in future printings.

Printed and bound in China

Acknowledgements

Each time I travel to a site and tell someone that I am writing an art travel guide, I am led to more art sites that I would not have known about—so, thanks to all those people who propelled me to the finish line.

I am grateful to the Folk Art Society of America for the annual tours they conduct in different parts of the country, which have taken me not only to many visionary sites but also to private collections I would have never been able to see without this organization.

I am grateful to two fellow travelers: Bev, who explored many California sites with me, and Diana, who chauffeured me up and down the East Coast.

Thanks to all the site directors who gave my colleagues and me tours and to all the participating venues who were so kind as to furnish a picture of their site for the book.

Thanks to Laura, our longtime designer, for all her helpful suggestions and final touches, to Dodie, who loves to work with words, and to our longtime proofreader Erica, who caught all those unseen typos.

And thanks to the readers, who allow us to provide them with our recommendations.

And, last but not least, a special thanks to all the artists who shared their artwork with the many museums and parks we visited.

Queen Califia's Magical Circle (on front cover)
Queen Califia's Magical Circle is Niki de Saint Phalle's only American sculpture garden and the last major international project created by her. The Circle, with a 400-foot-long undulating snake outlining its wall, was completed after her death in 2002. The garden has several totems reaching as high as 20 feet, benches from which you can gaze at the wondrous creatures, and a major sculpture of Queen Califia in the center. The site honors Queen Califia, the fictional black queen of the Amazon, whose name the Spaniards borrowed for their land, California. In Saint Phalle's depiction of Queen Califia, she stands atop a griffin-like beast holding a bird that shines in the sun. The bird-like figure has hatched a golden egg. Every inch of The Circle is covered in mosaic tiles, most individually designed and handmade: mother-of-pearl, abalone, agate, turquoise, malachite, tiger's eye, and carnelian pebbles of different shapes. Saint Phalle personally chose and intentionally planned placement of each tile on each sculpture—her workmanship is meticulous throughout. Children will love the playfulness of her choices and are encouraged to play on any of the sculptures.
Kit Carson Park, 333 Bear Valley Pkwy, Escondido, CA. 760.838.4691. queencalifia.org

Trees, 1986 by Terry Allen
Stuart Collection, UC San Diego (page 81)
Art Terry Allen
Licensed by VAGA, New York, NY
Photo by Becky Cohen

Introduction

Frank Gehry said, "There's a certain threat to taking a leap. Once you try it, you can't stop." That's exactly what happened to me some 25 years ago when I started researching contemporary art sites across the United States. I couldn't stop visiting these wonderful off-the-beaten-path venues. I explored because I was curious. My interest in sculpture, architecture and outsider art increased enormously during my travels. The more I studied, the more I yearned to travel again to these great spots. I thought my thirst would be quenched with one viewing of a site, but I was wrong. I was happy to take my friends along for their first visit.

Initially, as I was gathering data about the lesser-known art venues, I had no idea I would compile a book. Well into my travels, however, I decided that I wanted to introduce the public to these magical places, so I decided to put together this art travel guide.

This guide is for art lovers and explorers, spry and sedantary. Just reading and viewing the pictures becomes an adventure. I hope people will get so excited that they'll start an art project—maybe create an art car parade in their town, or a haute fashion show fundraiser, a plein air exhibition of rock sculpture in their garden, have a great time visiting a site, simply get inspired.

Choosing the "best" art sites around the country was not my aim. Instead, I searched for the most interesting off-the-beaten-path museums, sculpture parks, architecture, college art spaces, visionary sites—those hidden venues not listed in most travel guides.

As you visit these sites, please let them know that you discovered their venue through this travel guide. Email us—info@arttravelguide.info—your comments and suggestions about your favorite local, national and international art venues. I'm sure we've missed a lot! In fact, we're planning to publish a second volume with over 100 more, entirely new venues. A future international art travel guide, also in the making, will include Japan and Europe.

I hope you enjoy celebrating art as much as I have!

Snake Path, 1992 by Alexis Smith
Stuart Collection, UC San Diego (page 81)
Photo by Philipp Scholz Rittermann

What this book contains

The contents of this guide are divided into the categories listed below and in the Table of Contents. At the end of the book, you will find an alphabetical as well as a statewide index to help you plan your trips.

Sculpture parks have been around since Greek and Roman times; palaces had beautiful gardens with bronze and marble sculptures. Today, outdoor sculpture gardens are still an important part of our culture. There are over 200 sculpture parks across the United States, ranging from three to hundreds of acres; more appear annually. Events listed are one-of-a-kind celebrations that you won't want to miss in your travels.

With a focus on modern and contemporary art, I've listed museums that you might not usually be aware of and that often are not listed in generic travel guides.

Visionary sites have been created by laymen who generally don't call themselves artists. Many of these sites were created during the 50's and have been saved or rescued by present-day art lovers, presenting us with a glimpse into the past.

Even art enthusiasts overlook some fantastic art venues on college campuses: museums, galleries, sculpture parks and lots of public art installations. If your local university is not listed here, check it out online; you might be surprised at what art venues you'll find.

Art centers are places where you can watch artists at work and have the opportunity to talk with them, see how they think and buy new pieces for your art collection.

Architects listed in this book are among the most renowned and award-winning in the field today. Several have received the highly coveted Pritzker Prize. Three spectacular churches by great architects are included.

Earth works, sometimes called land art, came into their own in the 60's; you'll find two important surviving sites from that genre.

If you are interested in a particular medium—tiles, chalk, murals, glass, clay or plein air—explore the art media section.

Only a few favorite hotels and one restaurant are listed—the best of the best.

Dedicated to my darling daughter Hannah

Table of Contents

American Visionary Art Museum's (page 48) bird-themed sculpture plaza outside of The Jim Rouse Visonary Center (a former whiskey warehouse) at twilight featuring Andrew Logan's *Cosmic Space Egg*, Dr Evermor's *Phoenix* and *Bird's Nest Balcony* by David Hess. Photo by Paul Burk

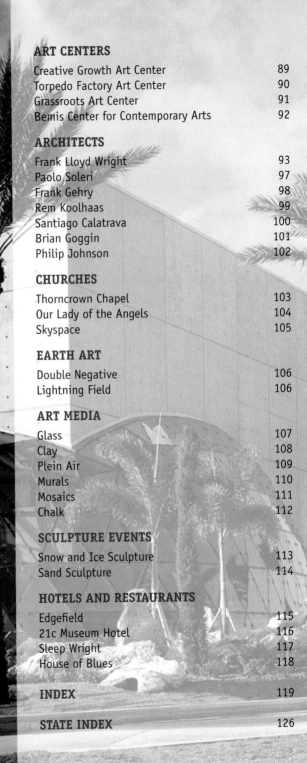

Exterior view of Dalí Museum (page 47)
Courtesy Dalí Museum

Mark di Suvero (front to back): *Mon Pere, Mon Pere*, 1973-75, steel, 35'x40'x40'4", *Mother Peace*, 1969-70, steel painted orange, 41'8"x49'5"x44'3". Storm King Art Center, Mountainville, NY. Photo by Jerry L Thompson.

Storm King Art Center, 50 miles north of New York City, turned 50 years old in 2011. The 500 acres—mowed lawns, fields and woodlands—provide the grounds for 120 sculptures by 100 internationally renowned artists: Abakanowicz, Aycock, Bourgeois, Calder, di Suvero, Moore, Nevelson, Grosvenor, Paik, von Rydingsvard, Noguchi, Serra, Talasnik and more. Emphasis is on abstract welded steel works from the 60's.

Maya Lin's third and final Wave Field is masterful. Nearby is Andy Goldsworthy's Wall, a 2278-foot-long serpentine dry wall, part of the landscape since 2000. Don't miss the surprisingly comfortable *Butterfly Chair* and *Nickel Couch* by Johnny Swing at the museum tram stop or George Cutts' Sea Change (fun to watch from the picnic tables at the cafe).

You'll want to hop on the tram to take you over the large acreage of wavelike hills and open skies with wonderful surprises wherever you gaze. Meandering trails and wooded groves make discovering sculpture a real pleasure.

The museum building contains nine exhibition galleries as well as a small bookstore.

Your kids will love Storm King too—interacting with di Suvero's gargantuan sculptures, hitting the gong with a special hammer. Plan to spend the entire day; bring a picnic lunch or enjoy the cafe. You'll do lots of walking, so wear comfortable shoes. Bike are also available to rent if you choose.

Mountainville, NY. 845.534.3115. stormkingartcenter.org

Aerial View 2. Courtesy Grounds for Sculpture.

Opened in 1992, this sculpture park not only keeps expanding its grounds, but also continues to add new sculptures annually: About 250 sculptures are presently exhibited. With two major indoor exhibit spaces and 35 landscaped acres outdoors, your visit can take from several hours to all day to navigate. Part of the grounds sit on a lake, where you will receive pleasant sculptural surprises. Often, sculpture parks have hidden and "to be found" spots, and there is no exception here. These grounds are easy to get lost in as you wander down secluded paths. You'll be gasping in amazement at some of the sculptures by well-known as well as emerging artists: Beasley, Abakanowicz, Bullock, Segal, Seward Johnson Jr, Pepper and more. Even if you don't recognize the artists by name, the sculptures are fantastic. As an added benefit for the seeing-impaired, sculptures have plaques that indicate whether or not they may be touched.

The organization backing this park publishes *Sculpture Magazine* and sponsors an annual Sculpture Symposium, which both sculptors and the public can attend. Interesting talks, new product information and tours of private and public collections are part of the conference.

A lecture series, artist-in-residence program (Patrick Dougherty in 2005), and an annual juried photography exhibition (relating to sculpture) also take place. This is one of the grandest spaces in the U.S. for the public to become educated about and experience sculpture.

→ Though you're in New Jersey, keep in mind you are minutes away from Philadelphia and New York sites.

18 Fairgrounds Rd, Hamilton, NJ. 609.586.0616. groundsforsculpture.org

The Eagle by Alexander Calder. Photo by Paul Warchol. ©2012 Calder Foundation, New York/Artists Rights Society (ARS), New York.

This sculpture park opened in 2007 and created a huge buzz within and without the art world. The magnificent views of Eliott Bay and the great works of art by leading masters—Smith, Pepper, Caro, Kelly, di Suvero, Serra, Bourgeois—on the nine-acre waterfront can't be beat. There is an outdoor amphitheater ready for performances; its centerpiece is Richard Serra's *Wake*—30 tons of huge, undulating steel plates. Calder's *The Eagle*, deep red, standing on the highest bluff of the park, focuses your attention out over the bay. Most fun of all is *Typewriter Eraser, Scale X* by Claes Oldenburg and Coosje van Bruggen, easily viewed by motorists scooting by on the highway. The long pathway and bridge that hold *Seattle Cloud Cover* by Teresita Fernandez are a special stretch of walk. Keep your eyes on the art (the colored glass) and you will see Seattle views in a new light. I almost missed *Split*—a towering stainless steel tree by Roxy Paine—which turned out to be my favorite piece of all. And, yes, what looks like a greenhouse at the corner of Broad and Elliott is an artwork entitled *Neukom Vivarium*—a hybrid of sculpture, architecture, environmental education and horticulture that connects art and science, by Mark Dion.

The pleasant cafe and indoor pavilion housing temporary exhibits will warm you if you're an early morning visitor, which, by the way, is one of the most pleasant and quietest times to take your hour-or-so stroll through the free-entry grounds.

2901 Western Ave & Broad St, Seattle, WA. 206.654.3100. seattleartmuseum.org

The Way. Visitors explore Alexander Liberman's monumental sculpture. Courtesy of Laumeier Sculpture Park.

An internationally-recognized open-air museum, this park's campus is 105 acres. Laumeier Sculpture Park collects, commissions and exhibits monumental contemporary sculpture, as well as site-specific and environmental sculpture. Over 75 pieces include works by Morris, von Rydingsvard, Shea, LeWitt, de Saint Phalle, Acconci, Pepper, Miss, Hamilton Finlay and more. Plan to spend several hours here walking the landscaped grounds and nature trails.

An indoor exhibition space that mounts three exhibitions annually is also on the property. The Maquettes for the Blind program opens the collection to sight-impaired guests by providing interpretive text in Braille.

Every year on Mother's Day weekend, 150 of the nation's best artists welcome over 18,000 visitors to the park during a three-day open-air art fair. The pool of juried artists exhibit and sell an impressive array of work in clay, fiber, glass, jewelry, mixed media, new media, painting, photography, printmaking, sculpture and wood.

12580 Rott Rd, St Louis, MO. 314.615.5278. laumeier.org

A group of parents and students enjoys a guided tour of the collection including Mark di Suvero's sculpture, *Bornibus*. Courtesy of Laumeier Sculpture Park.

Tower (DC) by Sol LeWitt, 1989-2009, concrete block and mortar, 15'11⅝"x4'7⅝"x4'7⅝". Courtesy of Barbara Krakow Gallery, Boston, MA and The Estate of Sol LeWitt. Funded by Museum supporters at the 2008 deCordova Annual Benefit. Photo by Chris Grimley.

You'll be impressed from the moment you enter the grounds and view *Laid* by Martha Friedman. Established in 1950, deCordova hosts more than 60 outdoor sculpture works at any given time: Jime Dine, Ronald Gonzales, Antony Gorley, Liberman, Lichtenstein, Paul Matisse, Nam June Paik, Steven Siegel, William Tucker, Ursula von Rydingsvard, Joseph Wheelwright and many more.

Inside the museum—the "castle"—you will find rotating exhibitions of contemporary American art. A permanent collection of approximately 3400 works is maintained.

DeCordova is committed to maintaining a strong relationship with established and emerging New England artists. During the 60's, deCordova organized outdoor sculpture exhibitions to introduce audiences to evolving large-scale Modernist sculpture. A 1966 exhibition included significant works by Calder, Rickey, Max Bill and Alexander Liberman.

You'll want to linger and have a picnic on a nice day; basket and blanket can be rented for $5 at the cafe. Over 125,000 visitors enjoy the 35 acres of grounds each year, which is open from dawn to dusk 365 days of the year. DeCordova offers one of the largest non-degree-granting studio art programs in New England, enrolling approximately 2000 students in various classes and workshops throughout the year.

→ About 10 minutes down the road, you can tour a National Historic Landmark—the Gropius House, home of Walter Gropius, founder of Bauhaus. I M Pei—one of his students—occasionally took care of the property when Gropius was on vacation. A one-hour tour is available by reservation: 781.259.8098. Use your ticket from DeCordova for free entry!

51 Sandy Pond Rd, Lincoln, MA. 781.259.8355. decordova.org

Dancers and Fold Square Alphabet Q. Courtesy Cedarhurst Center for the Arts.

Sculpture parks are places to spend time walking and inhaling the air and art. This is one of the better specimens in the U.S. in which to do so. Kuenz Sculpture Park, located on the grounds of Cedarhurst Center for the Arts, opened in 1992 on 90 acres of the estate of John R Mitchell. It exhibits approximately 50 pieces, some on temporary and some on permanent display; Oppenheim, Benton, Cavallaro and more are installed throughout

the acreage. John Kearny's *Gorilla*—made from chrome car bumpers—greets guests as they enter the property. Previously on loan was *Venus Verde*, a "dress" by Kathleen Holmes, and *Serendipity* by Chakaia Booker (tire scrap sculpture). A biennial sculpture competition brings in new work.

Visitors to Cedarhurst can also experience a variety of temporary exhibits throughout the year in the Beal Grand Corridor Gallery. In 2008, this new indoor exhibition center started highlighting more art from the Mitchells' collection: Sargent, Cassatt, Bellows, Eakins, Glackens, Henri, Davies, Prendergast, Hassam, and Luks, among others.

On Labor Day weekend, an annual craft fair with over 150 exhibitors is held.

Cedarhurst Center for the Arts, 2600 Richview Rd, Mt Vernon, IL. 618.242.1236. cedarhurst.org

Horse by John Kearney.
Courtesy Cedarhurst Center for the Arts.

Created in 1986 under the leadership of sculptor Mark di Suvero, this park is situated on the site of an abandoned riverside landfill. Today it is an internationally renowned outdoor museum and also has an artist-in-residence program.

The most permanent aspect of the park is change; thus, you'll see something new each time you visit. The park is adjacent to di Suvero's New York studio, where work in progress can often be seen.

FLOAT is a popular biennial exhibition of site-specific, temporary, interactive and ephemeral works that are installed throughout the park.

The five-acre park also serves as a venue for kite-flying events, fitness programs, a bike parade, a craft market and other special events.

With its to-die-for view of Manhattan and wonderfully inspiring sculptures, it's a venue that shouldn't be left unvisited when you go to the Big Apple.

3201 Vernon Blvd (@ Broadway), Long Island City, NY. 718.956.1819. socratessculpturepark.org

Courtesy Socrates Sculpture Park

Sculpture Center

The Sculpture Center is an organization founded in 1928 by Dorothea Denslow as "The Clay Club." Since 2002, it has been located in a former trolley repair shop, redesigned by artist and architect Maya Lin. It includes 6000 square feet of indoor and 3000 square feet of outdoor exhibition space. The Sculpture Center is dedicated to experimental and innovative developments in contemporary sculpture and to the exhibition of pioneering works by emerging and established national and international artists. With no permanent collection, the center focuses its efforts on commissioning and producing contemporary art.

→ Visit nearby PS 1 and Fisher Landau Center for the Arts (page 45), Socrates Sculpture Park (above) and Noguchi Museum (page 42).

4419 Purves St, Long Island City, NY. 718.361.1750. sculpture-center.org

Courtesy Benson Sculpture Park

In 1984, a group of five Loveland sculptors—George Lundeen, Dan Ostermiller, George Walbye, Fritz White, and Hollis Williford—together with representatives of the city of Loveland, the Chamber of Commerce and a few interested citizens, fostered the idea of a sculpture show in Benson Park.

They envisioned an annual outdoor exhibition and sale in a unique environment for sculptors from across the country to showcase their work, as well as a way to generate funding for a sculpture garden. In 1985, their dream became a reality. Each year, proceeds from the long-running (25-plus years) show go toward the purchase of a new sculpture for the garden. Benson Park's 10 acres now hold over 100 pieces: Goodacre, Ostermiller, Ullberg and more. This extraordinary collection of art is situated around a lagoon in the midst of trees, flowers and natural habitat areas, with the Rocky Mountains as a majestic backdrop.

The first annual *Sculpture in the Park* show had 50 local artists participating. Over 2000 people attended the show and purchased $50,000 worth of sculpture. Over the years, the show has expanded its diversity of artwork to include representational, stylized, and abstract sculpture in a variety of media: bronze, stone, wood, ceramic, glass, metal and mixed media. Sculpture in the Park, held in October, is now the largest outdoor juried sculpture show in the country with sales over $1 million and over 200 international artists exhibiting their work.

29th & Aspen Dr, Loveland, CO. 970.663.2940.
sculptureinthepark.org

Courtesy Benson Sculpture Park

Study in Heightened Perspective, a garden installation by Jack Lenor Larsen, is a centerpiece of the *Red Garden*. Photo courtesy of LongHouse Reserve.

On Long Island's beautiful South Shore sits a 16-acre garden unlike any other, a place where art and nature are woven together seamlessly—Jack Lenor Larsen's LongHouse Reserve. Lush grasses, colorful rhododendrons and azaleas, specimen trees and a lily-laden pond provide the setting for massive sculptures from the world's most recognized artists: Abakanowicz, Chihuly, de Kooning, Fuller, Lichtenstein, Lachaise, LeWitt, Rickey, and Takaezu, to name just a few.

Since Jack Lenor Larsen—weaver, fabric designer, gardener, art collector—acquired the property in 1975, he has created an entrance drive lined with majestic cryptomerias and established lawns and ornamental borders.

Fly's Eye Dome—a large geodesic dome by Buckminster Fuller—can be explored inside and out . . . a circle of frames to observe the sky and surrounding nature.

For this adventure, wear comfortable shoes and wide-brimmed hat; meander alone or with family and friends. Self-guided walking tours and a month-by-month perennial blossom brochure will help you enjoy your visit. Docent-led tours can be arranged. Twilight tours occur on specific evenings in late April through October.

A beautifully photographed book by Molly Chappellet—*Jack Lenor Larsen's LongHouse*—will give you an armchair ride through the grounds if you are unable to visit.

→ About 15 miles away, you can visit the Parrish Museum, dedicated to American art, with a focus on Long Island's East End artists.

33 Hands Creek Rd, East Hampton, NY. 631.329.3568. longhouse.org

The Tower by Ann Hamilton. Photo by Ann Hamilton.

This spectacular private reserve has 17 site-specific installations collected by the Olivers over a 20-year period. Mr Oliver himself will lead your group over the two-mile trek through natural flowing lands. You'll hear the amazing story of how his Serra piece was installed, and sit by the ranch's uniquely tiled pool high above the Russian River. You'll most likely end your trip by walking down

Bruce Nauman's site-specific staircase. Mr Oliver makes himself available to answer any questions about these unique and wonderful artworks.

Performances take place in the latest sculpture installation—*The Tower*, an eight-story concrete tower with a double-helix interior staircase designed by Ann Hamilton (above). Goldsworthy, Shea, Nauman, Serra, von Rydingsvard, Stackhouse . . . Wow! What a private collection. We're so lucky he shares this by allowing patrons of nonprofit art organizations to tour. What a unique method to share his love for art and, at the same time, help nonprofit art organizations raise funds.

Geyserville, CA. 510.412.9090 ext 203. Private tours only. To be part of a tour, search online under "oliver sculpture ranch" and you will get listings of organizations sponsoring tours. sculpture.org/documents/scmag02/oct02/oliver/oliver.shtml

Untitled by Martin Puryear.

Reclining Figure 1956 by Henry Moore. Courtesy PepsiCo. Reproduced by permission of the Henry Moore Foundation.

The beautifully terraced seven-building-headquarters of PepsiCo corporation was designed by Edward Durrell Stone, one of America's foremost architects. The buildings occupy 10 acres of the 144-acre complex, which includes a world-class sculpture collection.

Believing in the idea that art in the workplace can create innovation and stronger work ethics, Donald M Kendall, former Chairman of the Board and CEO of PepsiCo, conceived and brought into being these spectacular grounds—an integration of architecture, landscape and sculpture. Visiting will show you he was right—you'll wish you worked here! Intentional placement of both plant and sculpture is obvious throughout the landscape. Spring and summer bring out different aspects of the art and plants.

The gardens were originally designed by the world-famous landscape designer Russell Page and were extended by François Goffinet. Not until the 80's, however, was sculpture exhibited. You'll find 45 important large-scale pieces of bronze, marble, steel, nickel, resin, granite and spruce by 20th-century artists: Calder (*Hat's Off*), Dubuffet, Ernst, Laurens, Lipchitz, Lipton, Moore, Rodin, Giacometti, Pomodoro (my favorite), Oldenberg, Smith and more.

You'll have a fantastic day in the lush gardens, away from the hubbub of New York City, and it's free! Be sure to take off your shoes and let your toes stretch into the manicured lawn.

→ Neuberger Museum, designed by Philip Johnson, is directly across the street within the SUNY campus; special exhibits and permanent exhibitions are held.

PepsiCo, 700 Anderson Hill Rd, Purchase, NY. 914.253.3000. sirpepsi.com/pepsi1.htm

Tori by Bruce Johnson, 1984. Photo by Anthony Lindsey.

Founded by Carl Djerassi—author, playwright, and professor emeritus of chemistry at Stanford University—and recognized as one of the world's eminent artist residency programs, Djerassi has provided the gift of time to over 2000 artists from around the world. Over the years, many artists have left their mark across the acreage by installing sculptures—sometimes hidden, sometimes in full view—that now comprise the collection of more than 40 site-specific pieces: David Nash, Joyce Guatemala, Mauro Staccioli, Mark Reeves, Mel Henderson, John Roloff, Patrick Dougherty and others.

An old barn, which is retrofitted with plexi-panels in the new roof to imitate the dappled lighting of the old roof, is open to the public during the one-day-a-year Open House.

The private 580-acre ranch is breathtaking and serene. Morning hours on the ridge are quiet and misty with the sun filtering through the redwoods. Be prepared for rain or drizzles even in summer—you're walking on the coastal range through forests, creeks and blazing hot pastures. Walking shoes and jeans are appropriate for the rugged terrain. Plan to arrive earlier than your scheduled tour time, as you're apt to get lost finding this remote spot and you don't want to be late and miss your memorable tour! Surprises galore await you at this mystical site. Reservations required.

→ Visit nearby Stanford campus (pages 79-80) and all of its art delights.

Woodside, CA. 650.747.1250. djerassi.org

Boys Cry Too by Orly Genger 2009. Rope with latex paint, 107 yards in length. Courtesy the artist. Photo by Ross Willows.

This sculpture park has over 60 acres of rolling farmland, wetlands and wooded areas exhibiting 80 large-scale sculptures by internationally recognized artists: Lipski, Pepper, Highstein, Knowlton, Venet, Abakanowicz, Oppenheim, Unger and more. Approximately 10 new pieces are added to the park annually. Some of the pieces you will view were created by artists participating in the artist-in-residence program. Dedicated to the display of innovative artwork and pushing the limits of traditional notions of sculpture, the curators are actively committed to seeking conceptual sculptures that surprise and challenge viewers. Temporary exhibitions are also arranged by independent curators. A path for viewing the sculpture follows the edge of a natural pond surrounded by trees, providing a shaded backdrop to view the pieces. Bicycles are provided, if desired, to enjoy the park—"a good thing" with so many sculptures to view.

A spacious visitor center that includes a 1500-square-foot Charles Benenson Gallery displays paintings.

Omi International Arts Center,
1405 County Rte 22, Ghent, NY.
518.392.4747. artomi.org

Untitled by Robert Grosvenor 1968. Painted aluminum with steel support, 100 feet in length. Courtesy private collection.

Pearl at work. Photo by Dustin Shores.

All Pearl Fryar ever wanted to do was to have a nice yard and win "yard of the month" in his hometown of Bishopville. In the process he got so passionate about his garden that he couldn't stop adding and shaping plants; the last count was 300.

Visited annually by thousands of tourists, Fryar's topiary innovations have been featured many times on television specials and in dozens of magazines. A documentary—*A Man Named Pearl*—will give you perspective on his passion for sculpting greenery.

Starting with his own yard and a desire to design, he obtained "recycled" plants from his local nursery. Over time, he developed his signature style of sweeping, twisted, otherworldly, abstract shapes—something between *The Wizard of Oz* and *Dr Seuss*. On any given day, you'll find him high up on a ladder with his gas-powered hedge trimmer, getting just the right angle on that bush that he's been sculpting for years.

Most of the neighbors have been inspired by Pearl to trim their own plants in unusual ways. He has helped some of them do just that.

He also has a number of metal "junk art" sculptures that he has created from recycled materials—a true folk artist! Besides winning many awards, he was named South Carolina Ambassador for Economic Development in 2003.

145 Broad Acres Rd, Bishopville, SC. 803.484.6495. pearlfryar.com

Photo by Jean Grosser.

View of Alexander Liberman's *Aria* in the Sculpture Park at Frederik Meijer Gardens & Sculpture Park, Grand Rapids, MI. Photo courtesy of Frederik Meijer Gardens & Sculpture Park.

With both a world-renowned permanent collection and dynamic exhibition program, this 132-acre facility now features more than 200 works. Three temporary exhibitions occur annually—indoors as well as outdoors. Through the permanent collections and ongoing exhibitions, Meijer Gardens has developed a reputation as one of the most significant sculpture collections in the nation, with sculpture featured by Calder, Rodin, Degas, Lichtenstein, Segal, Maillol, Lipchitz, Moore, Nevelson, di Suvero, Abakanowicz, Rickey, Oldenburg, van Bruggen, Munoz, Beaumont, Bourgeois, Paladino and others. Natural settings connected by waterways, meandering paths and quiet walkways create the beautiful gardens.

There is also a suite of three galleries—a 4500-square-foot state-of-the-art indoor exhibition space opened in 2000. To date, exhibitions have ranged from large-scale presentations of modern masters such as Rodin, Picasso, and Moore to contemporary masters such as Caro and Richard Hunt. A special exhibit by Jim Dine was held in 2011.

→ Downtown Grand Rapids has over 40 sculpture pieces along the Riverwalk: Oppenheim, Kinnebrew, Calder, Maya Lin's *Ecliptic*, Otterness, di Suvera and more.

→ Grand Rapids Museum was designed by Kulapat Yantrasast, former apprentice to Tado Ando (page 54), who created a glass and concrete structure with reflecting pool from a renovated 1910 Federal Building.

→ The Urban Institute for Contemporary Arts' new facility is in Grand Rapids' central downtown area.

1000 E Beltline Ave NE, Grand Rapids, MI. 888.957.1580. meijergardens.org

Nasher Sculpture Center Garden. Photo by Timothy Hursley.

A peaceful oasis in the middle of a bustling city, this sculpture park opened in October 2003, funded by collector Raymond Nasher. World-class sculptures—about 30 works displayed outside, 80 inside—include Picasso, Matisse, de Kooning, Miró, Borofsky (*Walking to the Sky*), Dubuffet, Oldenburg, David Smith, Giacometti and others. *Tending, (Blue)* by James Turrell, is a free-standing Skyspace and the only site-specific work commissioned for the sculpture garden.

Visiting on Thursday will allow you to experience the works during the daytime, the Turrell Skyspace at sunset, and the illuminated sculpture garden during the evening.

The 55,000-square-foot indoor facility was designed by Renzo Piano, who won the Pritzker Prize for Architecture in 1998. Built on the concept of a "museum without a roof," the barrel-vaulted ceiling features delicate glass panes suspended atop narrow steel ribs supported by thin, stainless steel rods. The lower level opens onto the one-and-a-half acre terraced garden

→ Not to miss: Located on one side of this sculpture garden is The Meyerson Symphony Center, designed by I M Pei, and on the other, The Dallas Museum of Art.

2001 Flora St, Dallas, TX. 214.242.5100.
nashersculpturecenter.org

Nasher Sculpture Center at Night. Photo by Timothy Hursley.

Reclamation by Melanie VanHouten. Courtesy Franconia Sculpture Park.

This sculpture park was one of the best surprises during my visit to Minnesota. The 45-minute drive from Minneapolis was well worthwhile—it turned out to be a real find! A 20-acre site founded in 1996, it is located right off a busy highway next to the St Croix River. Each year, 40-plus artists are selected through a competitive application process to be part of the residency program, ultimately creating and exhibiting sculptures at the park. There are now over 85 large-scale contemporary sculptures to view on the grounds. Though the artists were unknown to me, the surprise of each fantastically innovative piece is what made the visit so enjoyable. The timing was perfect—late afternoon when the sun is shining at a lower angle, the birds are singing and the quiet is setting in. Be sure to check all the nooks of the forest space: Some sculptures are hidden along the outer pathways and you won't want to miss any pieces.

A nonprofit community arts organization, Franconia's mission is "To foster an inspiring environment for artists to expand their skills and promote the public education of three-dimensional art"—and it's a grand success! At the core of its programming is a commitment to make visual arts accessible to both artist and audience. Franconia enhances its ever-changing exhibitions with educational and outreach programming that includes weekly artist-led tours and "Kids Make Sculpture" workshops.

29836 St Croix Trl, Franconia, MN 55074. 651.257.6668. franconia.org

Euclids Cross by Michael Dunbar. Photo by Richard Batdorf.

Overlooking the Great Miami River, Pyramid Hill Sculpture Park is a 265-acre outdoor museum, combining the lure of nature with the dynamic presence of monumental art—a setting where landscape and art come together in natural meadows and woodlands. A great way to experience Pyramid Hill is by taking one of the freshly painted Art Carts right up to one of the 55-plus sculptures.

The newest addition to the park is the Ancient Sculpture Museum, which allows you to travel back in time, visiting Roman, Greek, Etruscan and Egyptian Empires. It houses over 60 pieces of sculpture, each piece more than 1000 years old.

You can also enjoy a tea room and wedding chapel on the property.

The Annual Pyramid Hill Art Fair takes place in late September. Over 70 artists from the tri-state area display and sell their artwork to more than 5000 visitors.

→ Two spots in nearby Cincinnati not to miss: Contemporary Arts Center designed by Zaha Hadid in 2003 and a 1999 building designed by Frank Gehry—the Vontz Center for Molecular Studies at University of Cincinnati.

→ Also nearby is Harry Andrew's Chateau Laroche (Loveland Castle), something you won't forget.

1763 Hamilton-Cleves Rd, State Route 128, Hamilton, OH. 513.887.9514. pyramidhill.org

Recreation of Arthur Rackman's 1908 illustration *Meeting of Oberon & Titania.* ©2011 Festival of Arts/Pageant of the Masters. Photo by Rick Lang.

This amazing event began over 77 years ago, the week after the Los Angeles Olympic games in 1932. Laguna Beach was attempting to attract tourists to its then-faltering town. *Living Pictures Show* was created by artist and vaudevillian Lolita Perine and was a small success. Three years later, Roy Ropp, another artist and construction worker, expanded the concept and renamed the event *The Spirit of the Masters.* Now called *Pageant of the Masters*, this one-of-a-kind spectacle lasts two months—July and August—and sells out early.

When the live music begins from the orchestra pit, the performers on stage freeze and become part of a "live painting." The entire presentation, lasting over two hours, is accented with unusual acoustics, live music and showmanship. About 30-40 familiar paintings are "enacted" during the evening. "How did they do that?" is a common question. Most of the actors (volunteers) within the "live painting" manage to not even twitch! The lighting and scenery production is so good that the "painting enactment" appears three-dimensional. On occasion, the actors intentionally move out of position, allowing the audience to see how the living painting is composed, which creates total amazement for the audience.

From bronze sculptures to Meissen china, Boticelli to Warhol, all are depicted with utmost refinement. Each year a different theme is played out. The traditional piece at the end is Leonardo's *Last Supper.*

Binoculars are helpful for seeing the details of each painting performance and can be rented outside the theatre. Arrive early for the pre-production entertainment: food, music and art at the Laguna Beach Festival of Artists, with some 145 artists selling two- and three-dimensional artwork on the grounds. Today, the Festival of Arts Permanent Collection, expanded annually through purchases made from the exhibiting artists' work, contains more than 300 pieces.

A most unique event!

650 Laguna Canyon Rd, Laguna Beach, CA. 800.487.3378. foapom.com

May 2011 Open Studios, studio of James Groleau. Photo by John Arbuckle.

Open Studios are when a group of visual artists invite the public to their art studio—usually a weekend-long event. Sometimes artists demonstrate their creative process as well as sell their art directly to the public. This type of event—selling directly from their art studios—has become popular throughout the country. Collectors love to visit artists at their studio, and artists love that they don't have to pay a gallery commission—a win win situation.

One of the first renovations of an old public building into artist studios—eight buildings in all—was at San Francisco's Hunters Point. The studios—previously army barracks—now house over 200 artists, all within easy strolling distance, perfect for an open studio event.

During Hunters Point Open Studio, a semi-annual event, it's easy to spend the entire day viewing art, chatting with the artists, or sitting in the sun enjoying the fantastic views of San Francisco Bay.

The layout of the main building is one long, straight hallway with about seven side halls (two floors). It was so crowded when I attended that you had to excuse yourself to pass by, both in the studios and hallways. Every studio I entered had a dazzling, professional presentation.

SOMA (somarts.org) provides a preview of this city-wide four-weekend event: a fundraiser and gallery exhibition, at which one example of artwork from each artist involved is displayed.

→ Wouldn't it be fun to go to an Open Studio event in Santa Fe (santafe.org) or New York City (efanyc.org/open-studios)? Well, it's possible! If you are planning a visit to an area of the country, look online for their "Citywide Open Studio Event." They occur in almost every U.S. city these days. It's a great way to explore an unfamiliar city.

.

1 Horn Ave, San Francisco, CA. shipyardartists.com

Atomic Dog sitting in front of The Orange Show. Photo by Larry Harris.

What the heck is an "art car?" If you don't know, you'll certainly find out during this weekend-long event. The Art Car Parade in Houston—the world capital of art cars—is the premier art car show in the nation, and also the oldest at 20-plus years. About 250 cars create a two-hour parade with 250,000 spectators on the second Saturday in May.

After the parade is over, you can get up close and see the immense amount of time, creativity and money involved in creating these cars—cupcakes, elephants, hamburgers, atomic dogs (above) and more—and chat with the creators.

→ Visit the Art Car Museum in Houston during this event. artcarmuseum.com

→ Visit Art Car World, a museum in Douglas, Arizona, dedicated to the celebration and preservation of this popular mobile art form. artcarworld.org

→ BMW has commissioned art cars from Haring, Calder (the first in 1975), Stella, Warhol, Rauschenberg, Chia, Hockney, Holzer, Lictenstein, Jeff Koons (2010) and others. en.wikipedia.org/wiki/BMW_Art_Car

→ A book and video by Harrod Blank entitled *Wild Wheels* show many fantastic creations, both by him and other art car fanatics.

→ Peruse the following sites to find out more about art car parades throughout the country: kentuckyartcarweekend.com; gypsymermaid.com; artcarfest.com; artcars.com; artcarparade.com; artcarcalendar.com; and seattleartcars.org.

The Orange Show Center for Visionary Art. 713.926.6368. orangeshow.org

Usually, between 40 and 70 sculptures—that's how the vehicles are referred to—are entered into an official race. Great efforts are made by contestants—businesses, families and friends—to create a sculpture that floats in water and drives on sand, pavement and mud. Most participants dress in costume to match their vehicle, and if not manning the vehicle, they run alongside it as mascots in the parade.

The World Championship—a triathlon of the art world—is held in Eureka, CA (kineticgrandchampionship.com). There are also quite a few other such races held within the U.S. annually: Ventura, CA (kineticrace. com); Corvallis, OR (davincidays.org); Klamath Falls, OR (klamathkinetic.org); East Coast Championship in Baltimore, MD (kineticbaltimore.com (page 48); Sheboygan, WI (www.jmkac.org (page 52); Port Townsend, WA (ptkineticrace.org); Boulder, CO (kineticists.org); and Philadelphia, PA (kinetickensington.org).

Traditionally, silly names are given to each of the contraptions/sculptures: "Basket Case," "Peregrine Emu," "Viking Ship," "Albino Rhinoceros," "Ten-foot Carrot," "Twins Crew" and "Mullet Bullet" are some examples.

Being an onlooker at a kinetic race event takes a lot of stamina—no exaggeration. Following the traveling sculptures' route to the different venues—water, pavement, sand, mud—will entail several miles of walking.

Kids between 11-15 enjoy the event immensely. Viewing the parade may lead them to participate in creating a sculpture in the future.

→ The Kinetic Sculpture Museum in Ferndale, California, exhibits machines from the past 35 Eureka competitions as well as a video of the local race.

Recycle Runway

Public artist and environmental educator Nancy Judd created Recycle Runway to educate us about conservation, using couture fashions that she designs from trash. Her elegant recycled fashion designs have been commissioned by companies such as Delta Air Lines®, Toyota®, Coca-Cola® and Target®. Environmental education takes place through public exhibitions, site-specific commissions and workshops. Find out more at www.recyclerunway.com.

Haute Trash Artists Collaborative

Artists involved with fashion show Haute Trash have spent hours picking through refuse in a variety of places—along the roadside, printers' offices, dumpsters, friends' garages—to bring you a haute couture runway show where everything is made from trash and recycled items. Haute Trash Artists Collaborative is a nonprofit that focuses on educating their audience while keeping them rolling in the aisles with tongue-in-cheek shows. You will never look at trash in the same way again—imagine a dress knitted from Nordstrom's bags, a gown made from aluminum can pop-tops, or a dress made from black handbags. Designers' aliases—Elvira Mental Werks, Prima Debris, Lotta Rubbish, The House of D'Trash, Toxic Blonde Productions, Sew Trashy—make for more fun.

The Nevada City, California-based collaborative has designer members from Los Angeles to San Francisco,

Skirt, armbands and top made from an employee's old shirt, accented with plastic Target bags. Paper beads created from cardboard product displays. Carmen Miranda-style headdress made with plastic bags, old cardboard displays and returned baseball game. One hundred hours in the making by Nancy Judd, 2002, commissioned by Target®.

Portland and Seattle. They present shows up and down the Western seaboard, as well as educational programs to schools. Check out their schedule at www.hautetrash.org.

Runaway Runway

Columbia Museum of Art in South Carolina has an annual Runaway Runway to raise funds as well as to bring environmental awareness through the use of post-consumer materials made into wildly fantastic wearables. Find out more at www.runawayrunway.net.

Shop Girl by Anna Villacorta of Ontario, Canada, Haute Trash Artists Collaborative. A tutu dress from specialty shopping bags. Photo by Rachel Olsson.

The Temple of Transition, an installation built by Chris Hankins, Diarmaid Horkan and the International Arts Megacrew at Burning Man 2011. Photo by Scott London. Burningman.com

In 1986, Larry Harvey and a friend built an eight-foot sculpture on Baker Beach in San Francisco. He lit the sculpture on fire to celebrate the summer solstice. In time, 800 people gathered in the sand and erected and burned another sculpture. Soon, 250 people cruised out to the Nevada desert to do the same. By 1994, some 1500 people were joining in. By 1997, with over 38,000 attendees, the "city in the desert"—Black Rock City, 160 miles outside Reno—was still growing. In 2010—its 25th year—over 50,000 participants came from around the world for the eight-day happening.

People wear costumes, create art installations, hold performances and live in the barren and remote desertland. Riding a bicycle or a registered art car (the only motor that can drive across the three-mile playa with 50-mile winds and brutally hot temperatures is not uncommon.

The finale of the eight days on the open playa is the burning of a 40-foot-tall wooden figure—Burning Man—that marks the center of the city.

There are several principles at Burning Man: No money is allowed to change hands in the attempt to create a society based on the giving of gifts; participation; leaving no trace when departing—you must leave your camp ground cleaner than when you arrived; communal effort; radical self-expression; and civic responsibility.

It is rare to have the pleasure of so many grand installations—300 or more—able to be viewed in one spot created by artists from so many walks of life. You can view scads of art from Burning Man online at www.images.burningman.com from the many previous years.

The Burning Man Experience (www.burningman.com) is just that: experiential. You need to attend the event and decide for yourself what it's about. It certainly will be unlike anything you've ever experienced before—a happening like no other!

The BabushCAN by Thornton Tomasseti. Photo by Kevin Wick.

"One **can** make a difference®" is Canstruction's® slogan. Canstruction® is a nonprofit organization and one of the most unique food charities in the world. It is the Society for Design Administration's community service project that promotes the design community and raises food for hunger relief efforts. Cheri Melillo, founder (1993), has worked tirelessly for the last 17 years to spread the vision and mission to over 140 cities across the U.S., Canada, Australia, and now the entire world.

Canstruction® holds annual "design-and-build" competitions in over 100 participating cities: Reno, Costa Mesa, San Antonio, Omaha, Minneapolis, Dallas, Santa Barbara, Houston, New York City and more. A team led by a professional in the design or construction industry—an architect, engineer, designer, contractor or professor of any of these disciplines—constructs giant-sized, fantastic sculptures, made entirely from unopened cans of food. The team funds the necessary cans through donations from manufacturers, distributors, grocery stores, team members and other means. In each city, after the structures are built and winners declared, the huge Canstruction®—built in a 12-16-hour day—is exhibited to the general public for a few days only. At the close of the exhibit, all of the cans used to build the structure are donated to a local food bank for distribution to community emergency feeding programs. The above Canstruction®—3472 cans, 1980 pounds of food—is nearly six feet tall and three feet in diameter. It helped feed nearly 2000 hungry New Yorkers tuna fish, peaches in pear juice, beef broth, vegetarian beans in tomato sauce, pork and beans in tomato sauce, pink beans and green beans.

View more amazing Canstruction® artworks from around the world at www.canstruction. org. See if your local city is involved in this food charity; contribute and enjoy an exhibit in person.

Zobop Fluoro, 2004, fluorescent tape, edition of 3, dimensions variable. ©Jim Lambie. Courtesy Sadie Coles HQ, London. Photo by Bruno.

The Goss-Michael Foundation, founded in 2007 by recording artist George Michael and his partner Kenny Goss, provides a forum for British contemporary art in the Dallas area. Splitting time between Dallas and London, Goss and Michael had become acquainted with many of the artists in the YBA (Young British Artists) movement. After two years of operating a gallery in Dallas, Goss and Michael decided to create a nonprofit art space for exhibiting works from their personal collection—Angus Fairhurst, Gilbert & George, Damien Hirst, Jim Lambie, Sarah Lucas, Adam McEwen, Jonathan Monk, Eva Rothschild and more.

The Goss-Michael Foundation offers the public a rotating schedule of exhibitions, changing quarterly. With each new exhibit, the foundation has the opportunity to partner with other institutions as well as individual artists. In an effort to keep exhibitions innovative, the artists are often invited to participate in the curatorial process and encouraged to produce new artwork specifically for the occasion. While on site, the artists participate in talks, tours, lectures, and performances that are often held in collaboration with other Dallas art institutions, offering the public the opportunity to learn about the art directly from the artist.

The Foundation has had the privilege of hosting many artists including Tracey Emin, Marc Quinn, James White, Tim Noble and Sue Webster, Michael Craig-Martin, Richard Patterson and Jeremy Deller.

→ Within a couple miles, you can visit both the MADI Museum (geometricmadimuseum. org) and Nasher Sculpture Center (page 28).

1405 Turtle Creek Blvd, Dallas, TX. 214.696.0555. gossmichaelfoundation.org

Donald Judd, 100 untitled works in mill aluminum, 1982-1986, detail. Permanent collection, The Chinati Foundation, Marfa, TX. Photo by Florian Holzherr, 2001.

Artist Donald Judd is creator of this destination museum to which viewers gladly travel hundreds of miles and sometimes take days to arrive.

A conceptual artist, he had a dream and made it happen. Judd wanted an alternative to a traditional museum—a permanent place to provide space for modern work. He searched long and hard and found an inexpensive venue—a 340-acre fort for sale in the middle of what used to be nowhere (and is still called that by some). Marfa, in the Texas high desert, has become part of the wonderful Chinati experience. The buildings he purchased go back to Pancho Villa and the Mexican-American War; many buildings at this location are pre-WWII. German POWs were housed here during WWII. Besides the original fort buildings, now called Chinati and named after the mountains in the surrounding area, Judd also bought several buildings in the small town of Marfa: the Block Cobb House, Whyte Building and more—15 spaces that include studios installed with artwork by Judd and others, living quarters, architecture offices and libraries.

Your tour of Chinati will show you work by Dan Flavin, John Chamberlain, Claes Oldenburg, and Carl Andre's One Hundred Sonnets (my favorite). I found out that the big 100 mill-aluminum boxes by Judd actually move in the heat of the day. You can see this by viewing the original plastic mats they were placed on. Some have moved as much as three inches—the amazing power of heat! You will also get to view Donald Judd's furniture. This small, desolate town of Marfa is beginning to boom with art-related venues. A remote town full of surprises—I almost decided to move there! I certainly hope to return and stay longer some day soon.

→ Donald Judd's home and studio in New York City is at 101 Spring St. Tours are available by reservation. Judd's studio was one of the founding sites in the program of Historic Artists' Homes and Studios for the National Trust for Historic Preservation. 212.219.2747 juddfoundation.org

104 S Highland Ave, Marfa, TX. 915.729.4362. chinati.org

Aerial view, Dia:Beacon, Riggio Galleries, 2002. Photo by Michael Govan. ©Dia Art Foundation.

This museum is heaven. A gargantuan space—240,000 square feet—allows for a crisp viewing of each artist exhibited: Martin, Nauman, Richter, Ryman, Smithson, Warhol, Judd, Chamberlain, Serra and more. Each artist has his own room; quite an honor.

Formerly a box printing facility, it is now the largest contemporary art museum in the Northeast. The lighting in most of the galleries is natural, enabling each piece of art to stand out. When you look down during your visit, you'll notice a beautiful wooden floor, marred in many places from past usage, exquisite in its refinishing and accented by the natural lighting.

Sol LeWitt's rooms are filled with wall scrawls—exquisitely detailed line drawings in muted tones that seem to create music. To be able to stand inside one of these rooms and absorb the soft images with natural light all by oneself is quite an emotional experience. The only way you'll be able to view *North, East, South, West 1967/2002* by Michael Heizer is by taking the 10:30 tour (reserve in advance).

There is so much to see here that it's easy to miss the basement, the upstairs and the west garden by Robert Irwin, with a sound piece by Lawler.

Because it's an hour-and-a-half train ride from the hubbub of New York City, plan to spend most of the day here. You won't regret it.

3 Beekman St, Beacon, NY. 845.440.0100. diabeacon.org

Courtesy The Bellagio

Though referred to as a gallery, this venue is really a museum. A museum in a hotel? The idea of a museum in a hotel created quite a buzz at the time when Steve Wynn owned the Bellagio. Many years later, this venue continues to bring great exhibits to Las Vegas: van Gogh, Renoir, Corot, Ansel Adams, Hockney and more. Be sure to buy your tickets in advance as this is a very popular spot.

Also, don't miss the extravagant Chihuly chandelier (right) located at the guest check-in at the Bellagio.

Outdoors you'll find the dancing (and singing) Fountains of Bellagio.

→ This museum is about an hour from Double Negative (page 106).

3600 Las Vegas Blvd S, Las Vegas, NV. 702.693.7871. bellagio.com/amenities/ gallery-of-fine-art.aspx

Courtesy The Bellagio

Photo by Elizabeth Felicella. Courtesy of The Noguchi Museum, NY.

This beautifully designed museum contains the work of its founder—son of an American writer and a Japanese poet—Isamu Noguchi. Noguchi received the National Medal of Arts in 1987. This museum opened in 1985, presenting a comprehensive collection of the artist's works in stone, metal, wood, and clay, as well as models for public projects and gardens, and Akari Light Sculptures. The museum is housed in 13 galleries within a converted factory building and encircles a garden containing major granite and basalt sculptures.

After a two-and-a-half-year-long renovation, the museum reopened in June 2004 with the addition of an education center, cafe, and shop. Although the renovated museum has a fresh look, great care has been taken to maintain the original character of the building, which was integral to Noguchi's vision. The raw industrial space of the former photo-engraving plant serves as a backdrop for the artist's sculpture.

It's a rare opportunity, and for me a favorite, to see a museum dedicated to one artist. Seeing many examples from an entire life of work always enhances understanding. Besides launching its first-ever program of temporary exhibitions, the museum has also created a special gallery devoted to Noguchi's celebrated work in interior design.

→ Catty-corner to this museum is Socrates Sculpture Park (page 19). A couple miles away are PS 1 and Fisher Landau Center for the Arts (page 45) as well as The Sculpture Center (page 19).

901 33rd Rd (at Vernon Blvd), Long Island City, NY. 718.204.7088. noguchi.org

Installation view from *How Soon Now* exhibition. Artwork by Nathalie Djurberg.

Don and Mera Rubell started one of the leading present-day contemporary art collections—The Rubell Family Collection—soon after they were married in 1964. Exhibited now in a converted 45,000- square-foot former DEA confiscated-goods warehouse, it has become a permanent museum for their extensive collection. Open to the public since 1996, the collection features exhibitions of work by such prominent artists as Maurizio Cattelan, Keith Haring, Damien Hirst, Anselm Kiefer, Jeff Koons, Paul McCarthy, Takashi Murakami, David Salle, Julian Schnabel and Cindy Sherman. The Rubell Family Collection has been recognized as the forerunner of what is often referred to as the "Miami model," in which private collectors create an independent forum to exhibit their collection. At a relatively young age, their son Jason and daughter Jennifer joined their parents in expanding the collection. In fact, Jason began his own personal art collection at the age of 14, initially financed by stringing tennis rackets after school.

Travelling exhibits are a part of the focus: Brooklyn Museum of Art and Palm Springs Art Museum are just two of the venues lucky enough to receive loans from the collection. Residents and travelers alike benefit from this Miami model—an experience in Miami you won't want to miss.

95 NW 29th St, Miami, FL. 305.573.6090. rubellfamilycollection.com

Installation view from *How Soon Now* exhibition. Artwork by Matthew Day Jackson.

Photo by Mike DeFilippo

What you'll find here is a 600,000-square-foot building—formerly the International Shoe Company—that has been converted into an eclectic playground for both adults and children. Found objects—old chimneys, salvaged bridges, construction cranes, abandoned airplanes and lots of tiles—have created this most unusual art space. Bob Cassilly, a classically trained sculptor, is the brain behind the museum.

I wished my six-year-old had been with me to enjoy the playground, enchanted caves, three-story slide, ball pit, renovated tree house, and sky tunnels. The playrooms are innovative and mysterious; younger children love the hidden tunnels and slides, The Water Pit, Skateless Park, and MonstroCity. An amazing 360-degree view of St Louis awaits you on the roof. While up there, take a seat behind the wheel of the famed school bus looming over the edge, right next to the 76-foot-long pencil sticking out of the window.

"Where the imagination runs wild" is the museum's logo, and rightly so. The creative reuse (such as printers' blocks that create a beautiful three-dimensional wallpaper) was invigorating and would exhilarate many a recycler.

Adults will appreciate the detailed mosaics and sculptures throughout the three floors and exterior playground.

Beatnik Bob's, a bohemian hangout, takes you back to the hippie era. World Aquarium will get you up-close to lots of creatures.

I remember reading about this museum before going to St Louis, thinking it looked quite interesting. I couldn't quite fit it into my mindset. Fortunately, I was able to fit it into my schedule and experience being a child for a day in this surrealistic palace until the three-story slide swished me back to the first floor and reality.

701 N 15th St, St Louis, MO. 314.231.2489. citymuseum.org

Founded by Alanna Heiss in 1971, this former public school has been the uncommon setting for diverse work for over 30 years. PS 1 is one of the oldest and largest nonprofit contemporary art institutions in the United States. It exhibits cutting-edge work—over 30 exhibits annually, including such artists as Abramovic, Barney, Basquiat, Darger, Nauman, and many others. Rather than collected work, you will find long-term installations: Turrell's Skyspace *Meeting* and works by Serra. Called "a true artistic laboratory" in its promos, this space will inspire you with the innovative exhibits by emerging and well-known artists. Allow about three hours to visit this former school with three floors of space, and take a break in the small cafe—one of the old schoolrooms.

→ A full day of art within a couple miles: PS 1, Fisher Landau Center for Art, The Noguchi Museum (page 42), Socrates Sculpture Park and The Sculpture Center (page 19).

2225 Jackson Ave (@ 46th Ave), Long Island City, NY. 718.784.2084. ps1.org

Portrait of Emily Fisher Landau by Andy Warhol, 1984.
©Andy Warhol Foundation for the Visual Arts, New York.

Fisher Landau Center for Art

This venue is a former parachute harness factory renovated into a three-story, 25,000-square-foot museum devoted to the contemporary art collection of Emily Fisher Landau. Many of the artworks were purchased early in the artists' careers—you'll see some surprising pieces you've not seen anywhere else: Gehry, Holzer, Martin, O'Keeffe, Rauschenberg, Ruscha, Kiki Smith, Twombly and Warhol.

38-27 30th St, Long Island City, NY.
718.937.0727. flcart.org

The Andy Warhol Museum, guests in Entrance Gallery

Here it is, all in one place: The artwork of one of the most influential American artists of the 20th century. This extensive permanent collection of Andy Warhol's life work—more than 900 paintings, 77 sculptures and collaborative works, 1500 drawings, 500 published and unique prints, and over 400 black-and-white photographs.

I've always liked museums that are dedicated to one artist, and this one, opened in 1994, is supreme. The collection provides an in-depth view of every period of Warhol's life, from the 40's through the 80's. With six floors of gallery space, you will view pieces that you have never seen before, even in a book—surprise after surprise.

→ Nearby visits to The Mattress Factory (page 46) and Fallingwater—Frank Lloyd Wright's most famous house (page 93)— will put you in bliss.

117 Sandusky St, Pittsburgh, PA. 412.237.8300. warhol.org

Andy Warhol, *Self-Portrait*, 1986, ©AWF

The new Dalí Museum opened in early 2011, attracting worldwide attention. Yann Weymouth conceived the museum's architectural design. *AOL Travel News* lists it as "one of the top buildings you have to see before you die." The museum's exterior features more than 900 triangular glass panels. This geodesic glass structure—*Glass Enigma*—is the only structure of its kind in North America, a 21st-century expression of Buckminster Fuller's geodesic dome as utilized in Dalí's Teatro Museo in Figueres, Spain.

The *Helical Staircase*—a spiral that ascends to the third-floor galleries—is the main architectural focus of the interior (right). Dalí recognized the helix as evidence of the divine in nature.

You'll be welcomed at the entrance by a visionary "Avant-Garden"—three distinct features: a misty grotto, a hedge labyrinth, and a patio with stone pavers demonstrating the harmonious proportions of the golden rectangle, marrying math, science, and art. The rocks reference Dalí's great love for the rock formations of his

Interior view of three-story helical staircase. Courtesy Dalí Museum. Photo by Dana Hoff.

native Cadaques, which he said embody the principle of metamorphosis. The grotto area is a passageway from the ordinary world to the surreal world inside the museum. To enter the museum, one must cross a bridge that parts the waters of the grotto pond.

Dalí's museum in his home town in Figueres, Spain, full of fun and whimsy, is the second most visited museum in that country. Every nook and cranny is a surprise. This museum in Florida proves its equal, both inside and out.

1 Dalí Blvd, St Petersburg, FL. 727.823.3767. thedali.org

Main building at dawn, featuring glittering mirrored mosaic walls. Photo by Dan Meyers.

If you love works created by self-taught artists (sometimes called outsiders, visionaries, or intuits), art that usually "dances" on the edge, this museum will enthrall you. Both the permanent collection and the temporary exhibits are outstanding.

The museum takes great care to educate the viewer. In the exhibition I saw, each artwork had a tag giving a short history of the artist's life, adding greatly to the viewing. Self-taught artists often use the unusual, perhaps recycled items, and you will see lots of that here. There were several pieces made with matchsticks—truly masterpieces, refined and exquisite. If you have any untapped urges to create, this museum will surely get you in the mood.

A newly added Tall Sculpture Barn houses larger items, including an art car. Located in the central plaza of the museum and viewable 24/7 is a giant 55-foot-tall, multicolored, wind-powered whirligig created by 76-year-old mechanic, farmer, and visionary artist Vollis Simpson.

The architecture of this museum is enhanced by mosaic shards of glass and mirrored tiles, shining brightly in the sun, creating a view from the road that is eye-catching, shiny and unusual. Most of the mosaic work is part of The Community Mosaic Wall Project—an arts apprenticeship program that provides hands-on art experience with mentorship by accomplished artists to over 250 of Baltimore's youth, who hand-made each of the mosaic panels adorning the exterior walls of the museum. What a cool way to involve the community! Kudos! Plans are for all of the concrete surfaces on the exterior of the museum's main building to be covered in mosaic eventually.

This museum is sponsor of the annual East Coast Championship Kinetic Races in April—a 30-year tradition (page 34). In late July, the museum also sponsors an art car show. A bizarre and fun collection of embellished autos can be viewed (page 33).

The museum shop has original visionary art that can be purchased, as well as books and other items. The cafe's exotic menu is accented by the spectacular view of the harbor.

800 Key Hwy, Baltimore, MD. 410.244.1900. avam.org

CIFO facade—4800 square feet of multicolored Bisazza tiles creating a bamboo motif. Photo courtesy Cisneros Fontanals Art Foundation.

Cisneros Fontanals Art Foundation is a nonprofit organization established in 2002 by Ella Fontanals-Cisneros to support artists who are exploring new directions in contemporary art.

Fontanals-Cisneros began collecting art in the early 70's, with a primary interest in works by Latin Americans: Lygia Clark, Waldemar Cordeiro, Jose Pedro Costigliolo, Carlos Cruz-Diez, Manuel Espinosa, Gego, Mathias Goeritz, Carmen Herrera, Alfredo Hlito, Ana Maria Maiolino, Alejandro Otero, Lygia Pape, Lidy Prati, Mira Schendel and Jesus Soto, among many others. The collection also includes a growing body of international contemporary art: Francys Alÿs, Sophie Calle, Mark Dion, Tracy Emin, Thomas Hirschorn, Jenny Holzer, Anish Kapoor, Subdoh Gupta,

William Kentridge, Vik Muniz (see his DVD *Waste Land*), Gabriel Orozco, Ernesto Neto, Guillermo Kuitca and Shirin Neshat as well as Lucio Fontana, Barbara Hepworth, Roberto Matta, Joaquin Torres-Garcia, Maria Freire and others. CIFO Art Space presents contemporary art exhibitions from the Ella Fontanals-Cisneros Collection in December, coinciding with Art Basel Miami.

The 1936 warehouse that houses this venue underwent a dramatic redesign before it opened. Fontanals-Cisneros joined efforts with architect Rene Gonzalez to create a warm and vibrant environment. The building's dramatic facade evokes nature and artistry. More than 200 colors were used in the extraordinary mosaic covering the facade (above).

1018 N Miami Ave, Miami, FL. 305.455.3380. cifo.org

Tree Logic by Natalie Jeremijenko. Photo by Kevin Kennefick.

The grounds at MASSMoCA formerly housed a vast complex of 19th-century factory buildings. With 13 acres, occupying nearly one-third of the city's downtown business district, it is the largest center for contemporary arts in the United States. Open since 1999, MASSMoCA has become one of the world's premier centers for creating—several artists have residencies at any given time—and exhibiting the best art of our time. With an annual attendance of over 120,000, it ranks among the most visited institutions dedicated to contemporary art in the United States. The museum thrives on art that is avant-garde and challenging, representing work by many of the most important artists of today, both well-known and emerging—Petah Coyne, Sol LeWitt, Don Gummer, David Byrne, Tony Oursler, Robert Rauschenberg and more. With huge, industrial-size galleries of 110,000 square feet and 19 galleries or more, large-scale installations can be created. Kidspace is a contemporary art gallery, studio, and educational program for children, located within the facilities.

Sol LeWitt: A Wall Drawing Retrospective is on view through 2033!

→ When you're in the area, also visit nearby venues: The Norman Rockwell Museum (nrm. org), Williams College Museum of Art (wcma. williams.edu), and the Clark Art Institute (clarkart.edu).

1040 Mass MoCA Wy, North Adams, MA. 413.662.2111. massmoca.org

Courtesy Frederick R Weisman Art Foundation. Photo by David Moore.

In 1982, Frederick Weisman purchased this Mediterranean-style estate to serve as his home and ultimately as a showcase for his personal collection of 20th-century art, which includes hand-painted ceilings, stucco details, and inlaid-wood floors. The private collection of contemporary artwork that now belongs to the Weisman Art Foundation remains at the estate exactly as Weisman displayed it; some original pieces even remain on the ceiling. In 1991, an annex (above) was added to accommodate larger-scale works.

The collection has approximately 500 pieces on display: Botero, Noguchi, Moore, Léger, Picasso, Warhol, Motherwell, Giacometti (both brothers), Klee, Brancusi, Hockney, Albers, Hofmann, Still, Johns, Miró, de Kooning, Francis, Rothko, Dubuffet, Dine, Bacon, Ernst, Rivers, Frankenthaler, Haring, Wesselmann, Oldenburg, Stella, Magritte, Ruscha, Albuquerque, Pollock, Kelly, Smith, Calder, Judd, and Rosenquist.

Since the estate is not located in a commercial zone, tours are small. All visitors must park in the driveway. Specific directions are given to you when reservations are confirmed. Your tour of the house, garden, and annex will be given by well-informed docents.

This is an outstanding collection—truly overwhelming—that many art lovers overlook when visiting southern California. Don't! As I write this, I remember what a treat it was—and I can't wait to return.

Los Angeles, CA. 310.277.5321. weismanfoundation.org

(Re)Possessed (installation view, John Michael Kohler Arts Center), by Xenobia Bailey, 1999-2009. Courtesy of the artist. Photo by Jeff Machtig, John Michael Kohler Arts Center.

"Expect the unexpected" is the tag line of this museum—a 40-year-old arts center devoted to self-taught artists, contemporary art, and folk art preservation. With changing exhibits throughout the year, this arts center functions as a catalyst for and explorer of new art forms and new ideas.

Selected sculpture pieces by Carl Peterson and Dr Evermor (page 67) are permanently installed in the center's gardens.

Don't miss the six washrooms—the first commissioned works undertaken by the center as part of a 1999 expansion. Emerging and mid-career artists have created examples of the center's philosophy: Art can enrich and inform every facet of our lives.

Part of the Arts Center's collection is Loy Allen Bowlin's modest Mississippi home, as well as personal effects. The self-declared "Original Rhinestone Cowboy" used hundreds of thousands of painstakingly applied dots of glitter, combined with paint, foil, photographs, and holiday decorations, to alter his residence as well as his dazzling cowboy suits. Also in the collection are Emery Blagdon, Nek Chand, Nick Engelbert, Mary Nohl, Eugene Von Bruenchenhein and Sam Rodia. The center was able to acquire one of few existing known works predating the legendary Watts Towers (page 63), made for the home of Rodia's former boss.

An Independence Day Art Armada shows off artistic and extraordinary boats in kinetic art races (page 34). A midsummer festival occurs in July, with over 135 exhibiting artists. Various art classes are offered for all ages.

608 New York Ave, Sheboygan, WI. 920.458.6144. jmkac.org

The Phillips Collection

This, America's first museum of modern art, opened in 1921. It displays selections by European and American masters from the 19th century to the present, including Pierre Auguste Renoir, Edgar Degas, Paul Klee, Henri Matisse, Claude Monet, Pablo Picasso, Vincent van Gogh, Maurice Prendergast, Mark Rothko, Paul Gauguin, Georgia O'Keeffe, Jacob Lawrence, and Richard Diebenkorn. The famous *The Luncheon of the Boating Party* by Renoir has a permanent home here too. Truly, this is one of the world's finest museums and overlooked by many tourists.

1600 21st St NW (at Q), Washington, DC. 202.387.2151. phillipscollection.org

Courtesy The Phillips Collection. Photo by Robert Lautman.

Kreeger Museum

This museum is located in the former residence of David and Carmen Kreeger, designed by renowned architect Philip Johnson—one of his early forays into postmodernism. Johnson was asked to create a structure that was a residence, gallery, and concert hall, all in one. Today it showcases the Kreegers' permanent collection of 19th- and 20th-century paintings and sculptures: Renoir, Gauguin, Sisley, Rodin, Picasso, Bonnard, Chagall, Redon, van Gogh, de Stael, Still, Beckmann, Dubuffet, Avery, Gorky, Miró, Monet, Stella, Courbet, Corot, Cezanne, Chagall, Munch, Braque, Kandinsky, Koons, Hofmann, Rosenquist, Calder, Smith, Brancusi, Albers, Degas, Léger, Modigliani, Mondrian, Pissarro, Ray, Tanguy, Gilliam, Moore, Arp, Maillol, Lipchitz, and Noguchi. This is truly an amazing venue that many tourists miss.

2401 Foxhall Rd NW, Washington, DC. 202.338.3552. kreegermuseum.org

Courtesy Kreeger Museum. Photo by Franko Khoury.

Water Court by Tadao Ando. Photo by Robert Pettus.
©Pulitzer Foundation for the Arts

Designed by Japanese 1995 Pritzker-prize winning architect Tadao Ando, this building is a serene, minimal setting for the contemplation of art. Past exhibits have included Picasso, Matisse, Lichtenstein, Warhol, Beckmann, Long, Oldenburg, Tuttle, Twombly, Sherman, and others. The Pulitzer possesses some of the same characteristics of a traditional museum: It has galleries that are open to the public, it presents changing exhibitions, and it aims to educate the public in various facets of the arts. However, the Pulitzer is a non-collecting institution whose mission also focuses on presenting programs that explore the interrelationship of art and architecture and allow a personalized experience with the arts.

Why are there no labels or wall texts? The Pulitzer encourages a direct and contemplative viewing experience with the artworks, almost as if you were living with them. Labels and text can aesthetically interfere with this immediate visual experience. (A visitor handout is available listing titles and information.)

→ Plan to visit the Contemporary Museum, next door, on the same day.

3716 Washington Blvd, St Louis, MO.
314.754.1848. pulitzerarts.org

Blue Black by Ellsworth Kelly
Photo by Robert Pettus
©Pulitzer Foundation for the Arts

South Facade

The Sioux City Art Center, founded in 1938 as a WPA project, has served as a cultural focus for Western Iowa and the surrounding region for more than 70 years. A program of acquisition of work by national and international artists has been underway during that entire period.

Designed by Skidmore, Owings, and Merrill, the 1997 addition—glass block art deco—houses a permanent collection with over 1000 works: William Bailey, Thomas Hart Benton, Dale Chihuly, John Steuart Curry, Salvador Dalí, John Henry, Kollwitz, Motherwell, Oldenburg, Paschke, Pearlstein, Riley, Uelsmann, Hockney, Whistler, and more.

Grant Wood's *Corn Room* mural is on extended exhibition in a special room constructed just for this exhibit. It holds one of the original pieces painted for Eppley's Martin Hotel dining room in Sioux City.

The primary intent from inception was to support living artists from Iowa and the greater Midwest through exhibitions and collecting. Temporary exhibitions grace the center, which presents local, national, and international artists, as well as occasional blockbuster touring shows.

ArtSplash is a juried outdoor show exhibiting work by 100 visual artists, held over Labor Day weekend—an annual event since 1994. Over 35,000 people attend the festival, visiting the Art Center and downtown Sioux City.

→ One-and-a-half hours south is Omaha, where you can visit the Bemis Center for Contemporary Arts (page 92) and the Joslyn Art Museum.

225 Nebraska St, Sioux City, IA. 712.279.6272. siouxcityartcenter.org

Courtesy SITE Santa Fe. Photo by Herbert Lotz.

SITE Santa Fe is a private nonprofit, non-collecting contemporary arts organization committed to enriching the cultural life of Santa Fe residents and visitors, providing an ongoing venue for exhibitions of artists who merit international recognition, as well as offering education and multidisciplinary public programs. SITE Santa Fe—sometimes referred to as SITE—is committed to exhibiting and exploring risk-taking art and is at the forefront of contemporary art presentation in this country and abroad. Some artists who have exhibited at SITE in the past include Janine Antoni, Teresita Fernandez, Andy Goldsworthy, Steina and Gary Simmons. Since it opened in 1995 with its first International Biennial, it has earned a stellar reputation. The International Biennial, now in its 9th year, is a crucial part of its mission. The biennial exhibits have also proven to be greatly successful and widely recognized and have featured contributions from world-famous artists such as Elizabeth Peyton, Marina Abramovic, Cai Guo-Qiang, Jo Baer, Takashi Murakami, Louise Bourgeois, Bridget Riley, Ed Ruscha, Jasper Johns, Jennifer Bartlett, Ellsworth Kelly, Francis Alÿs, Bruce Nauman, and more—a biennial event not to be missed.

→ While in Santa Fe, don't miss the Museum of International Folk Art (moifa.org); the Center for Contemporary Arts (ccasantafe.org); and the Georgia O'Keeffe Museum (okeeffemuseum.org).

1606 Paseo de Peralta, Santa Fe, NM. 505.989.1199. sitesantafe.or

Woman in the Moon by Robert Hudson, 1987. Photo by Ann Trinca.

This 217-acre nature reserve represents within its galleries and hillsides over 750 Bay Area artists: 2000-plus pieces of art, including a big red car hanging upside down from a tree. Tours begin in a huge barn-like structure built especially for this private collection. You will not find many "flower paintings" here; I saw exactly one. You will see a Gaudi-like art car from the 60's by David Best and ceramics by Robert Arneson, as well as whimsical pieces with unusual frames by Roy De Forest. One audio piece recited monotone comments as visitors walked by: "I'll never leave you. We belong together. You're gentle. I wish you were dead. I'll always love you." You'll see a rendition of the sunlight pouring through the stained glass at Chartres Cathedral: In 12 minutes the light rotates through an entire day of light. If you take the outdoor tour, you'll see *Untitled, (Minuet in MG)* by Samuel Yates—a seven-story skyscraper (65 feet high) made out of filing cabinets. Don't fear! If you happen to be standing near it on a day when the earth quakes, this piece has been built to withstand a quake. Works by Viola Frey, Mark di Suvero, Veronica di Rosa, William T Wiley, Paul Kos and others await your visit.

Local Color: The di Rosa Collection of Contemporary California Art—a book about the museum—is a great souvenir of this outstanding experience.

→ Visit the nearby Hess Collection (page 61)—outstanding.

5200 Sonoma Hwy, Napa, CA. 707.226.5991. dirosaart.org

Photo by by Cheri Eisenberg

This small but distinctive space does a great job of exhibiting superb works from outsider artists—some of the best I've seen. The organization has received gifts of works by William Hawkins, William Dawson, Minnie Evans, Howard Finster, Dwight Mackintosh, PM Wentworth, Wesley Willis, Joseph Yoakum and others. There is also a Henry Darger Room showing how the artist lived and worked.

The museum sponsors an annual show in November—The Intuit Show of Folk and Outsider Art—bringing dealers from across the country to exhibit. This is an event not to be missed if you like outsider art. The museum also offers lectures on outsider, intuitive, and visionary artists on a regular basis. Private tours to collectors' homes are also organized for members.

756 N Milwaukee, Chicago, IL. 312.243.9088. art.org

Smart Museum of Art

A must see, this wonderful museum with great shows makes you wonder why there are not more people browsing the galleries. The collection includes beautiful examples of Lipchitz, Rothko, Moore, Dove, Arp, The Chicago Imagists, Matta and more.

5550 S Greenwood Ave, Chicago, IL. 773.702.0200. smartmuseum.uchicago.edu

Exterior with a view of Richard Hunt's sculpture *Why* (1974). Courtesy Smart Museum of Art, The University of Chicago.

Magdalena Abakanowicz, *Standing Figures (Thirty)*, 1994-1998. Photo by Mark McDonald, Courtesy of The Nelson-Atkins Museum of Art.

The Nelson-Atkins Museum houses major contemporary works of Expressionist, Fauve, Cubist, Bauhaus, Dada and Surrealist art from the 1900-1945 era. Artists include de Kooning, Rothko, Pollock, David Smith, Diebenkorn, Estes, Duane Hanson, Warhol, Rauschenberg, Oldenburg, Judd, LeWitt, Agnes Martin, Bridget Riley, Martin Puryear, Butterfield, Elizabeth Murray, Anish Kapoor and others. The newer Bloch Building (below) was designed by Steven Holl.

The Kansas City Sculpture Park opened in 1989 at the museum. The 22-acre oasis has more than 30 sculptures including work by Abakanowicz, Lipchitz, Oldenburg, Shea, von Rydingsvard, Renoir, Shapiro, Calder, Segal, de Maria's site-specific *One Sun/34 Moons* and over 50 works by Henry Moore. Noguchi Sculpture Court exhibits seven sculptures by Isamu Noguchi, installed in a large, zen-inspired space.

4525 Oak St, Kansas City, MO.
816.751.1278.
nelson-atkins.org

View of the Bloch Building from Rockhill Road (east). Photo by Timothy Hursley. Courtesy of The Nelson-Atkins Museum of Art ©2006.

Infinity Dots Mirrored Room, 1996 by Yayoi Kusama. Photo by John Charley.

The Mattress Factory could be considered an idea lab for artists. A museum of contemporary art, it commissions site-specific works and maintains selected room-size installations in a permanent collection. It has exhibited new works created on the museum premises by over 300 artists from around the world through a residency program. There are 16 permanent installations on continuous display, including important works by James Turrell, Greer Lankton, Bill Woodrow, Allan Wexler, Jene Highstein, Winifred Lutz, William Anastasi, and Rolf Julius. It is a truly fun, innovative and inspiring environment. *Installations*, a great book and preparation for your visit, will give you an overview of the installations exhibited at The Mattress Factory in the 90's.

→ Don't miss the nearby Warhol Museum (page 46).

500 Sampsonia St, Pittsburgh, PA. 412.231.3169. mattress.org

Donald Hess standing in the gallery: *Johanna II* by Franz Gertsch on left. Courtesy Hess Collection.

The winding road leading to the Hess Winery is a serene drive. When you arrive at the quiet parking lot, you see contemporary sculptures displayed in the small, meadow courtyard garden, preparing you for the two-story exhibition space indoors.

Works collected by Donald Hess span the latter half of the 20th century. Each artist—Francis Bacon, Robert Motherwell, Frank Stella, Magdalena Abakanowicz and others—has more than one piece exhibited in his "corner" of the gallery, many from times in their careers with which I was not familiar. Viewing two to eight pieces from an artist's life work gives viewers more insight into that artist's mission—a rare treat. The auras of the artists even seem to be present.

One of the most powerful rooms is that of Franz Gertsch, a Swiss artist who creates extra-large realistic portraits as well as woodcut prints. The process of inking and rubbing these monumental print blocks involves the help of eight assistants, often taking six to twelve months to complete. You can purchase a book, found only at this gift store, that explains Gertsch's process.

My favorite piece in the collection is *Samba fur Johnny* by Marcus Raetz—60 eucalyptus leaves mounted on the wall with straight pins. There's lots of unusually wonderful work to view here in the quiet galleries.

I became so mesmerized with the exhibits that I forgot to buy or even partake of the wine—that's how good this collection is!

→ Don't miss the nearby Di Rosa (page 57), Napa Valley Museum, and Quixote Winery—the latter is designed by Austrian architect Friedensreich Hundertwasser.

4411 Redwood Rd, Napa, CA. 707.255.1144. hesscollection.com

The Firebird by Niki de Saint Phalle. Courtesy Bechtler Museum of Modern Art. Photo by Gary O'Brien. ©2012 Niki Charitable Art Foundation. All rights reserved / ARS, NY / ADAGP, Paris.

After inheriting a portion of his parents' mid-century modern art collection—Giacometti, Tinguely, Sam Francis, Nicholson, Mark Tobey, Paul Klee, Rouault, Le Corbusier, Hepworth, Picasso (*La Femme au Chapeau/Woman In a Hat*), Miró, de Stael, Warhol, Ernst, Léger, Vasarely—Andreas Bechtler made plans for a museum that would honor not only the art but also the way in which it was collected. His desire to share the collection amassed by the Bechtler family over 70 years with his adopted Charlotte, North Carolina, home, was fueled by his family's passion and commitment for collecting art and supporting artists.

Until the museum's opening in January 2010, the collection was privately held. Only a handful of the artworks in the Bechtler collection had ever been on public view in the United States.

The museum itself was designed by world-renowned Swiss architect (and Andreas Bechtler's fellow countryman) Mario Botta. The power of Botta's design connects it to the power of the art inside. The four-story 36,500-square-foot structure with its soaring glass atrium provides natural light throughout the galleries.

The Bechtler Museum of Modern Art is dedicated to the strongest aspects of mid-century modernism. The collection comprises more than 1400 works by 20th-century modern artists, mostly European. Some works are accompanied by books, photographs, and letters illustrating personal connections to the Bechtler family. The exterior (above) sports *The Firebird*, a 17-foot sculpture of mirrored and colored glass by Niki de Saint Phalle.

420 S Tryon St, Charlotte, NC. 704.353.9200. bechtler.org

This is by far the most famous West Coast visionary site. It was also the first visionary site successfully saved from demolition and, thus, received a lot of publicity.

The site was constructed entirely by one person's labor. Italian brick-layer Sam Rodia devoted 30-plus years of his life to the Towers. He just couldn't stop working on it, creating for himself a phantasmagorical landscape that would attract worldwide interest.

Mostly remembered for the Watts Riots of 1965, this area of Los Angeles was countryside when Rodia lived there. I was expecting to find it in the middle of a vast dust field. Lo and behold, it was on a block of houses surrounded by a new art center and park.

Rodia purchased his rectangular lot— shaped rather like a boat—in 1921. Improvising without a specific plan, he took objects and embedded them into various sculptures, creating a mosaic effect: recycled tiles, pottery, glass, sea shells, the ever-popular blue

Photo by Robert Berger

Milk of Magnesia bottle, green Seven-Up bottles, and more. Amongst the beautiful laid tiles, he designed a fountain and three vast towers, entwined with spirals and decorative stones. He called his creation *Nuestro Pueblo*—Our Town. In 1955, at 75, Rodia deeded his property to his neighbor and left town. The next year, a fire ruined the house; the Department of Building and Safety ordered it demolished. Through a group of local citizens, the towers were saved and proven safe. Since that time, extensive restoration has been conducted by the City of Los Angeles. Watts Towers has become a State Historic Park administered by the City of Los Angeles. Over $1 million from the U.S. Federal Emergency Management Agency was used to restore this site after the 1994 Los Angeles earthquake. It receives over 20,000 visitors a year. It is a stirring monument.

1765 E 107th St, Los Angeles, CA. 213.847.4646. wattstowers.us

Skylighted kitchen.
Photo courtesy of Forestiere
Underground Gardens LLC.

When I mentioned to my 93-year-old aunt in 2000 that I had just visited Forestiere Underground Gardens, she started reminiscing about her visit back in the 50's. Baldasare Forestiere—a Sicilian immigrant—helped dig the Boston subway as well as the NYC/NJ tunnel in 1901. He began hand-sculpting his own subterranean home in 1906 (the year of the famous San Francisco Earthquake). If you've experienced the weather in Fresno in summer, you will understand why he wanted an underground home and how great it felt on a 100-degree day to cook in his underground kitchen. Ultimately, his home had 100 rooms, many sculpted arches, and an 800-foot-long auto tunnel. In 1979, this site became a California Historical Landmark. It is also listed by the Department of Interior in the National Register of Historic Places, quite an honor for an individual's life work.

This site is reminiscent of Gaudi's Guell Park, Barcelona, without the elaborate mosaics that Gaudi incorporated. To support the earth above, Forestiere carved Roman arches, columns, and domes. Mortar and cement were used not only for structural purposes but also for beautification of the seven acres of underground rooms. Trees were planted underground and pop out through skylights he carved specifically for that purpose. A fish pond and foot bridge were also created.

An awesome and endearing creation, his house is still owned by his relatives. Your guided tour will be led by one or more of them!

5021 W Shaw Ave, Fresno, CA. 559.271.0734. undergroundgardens.com

Courtesy Paradise Gardens

Howard Finster, who died in 2001, is probably the best-known folk artist of our time. He has had exhibits throughout the world, including at the Smithsonian Institute. His work is in the permanent collection at the High Museum in Atlanta. His face graced the cover of the *The Wall Street Journal* and he has been featured in innumerable magazines and newspapers: *Time, Life, Southern Living, The New York Times, Chicago Sun-Times, Rolling Stone,* and *People.* He was on the "Tonight Show," "Good Morning America," and TV broadcasts in Canada, England, and Japan. He created album covers for well-known rock musicians REM and Talking Heads. The Coca-Cola company even commissioned Finster to paint an eight-foot-high Coke bottle to represent the United States at the 1996 Olympics in Georgia, his home state.

His main work of art, however, is Paradise Gardens, a site on four acres of land. The garden was begun in 1961 when he received a vision telling him to create sacred art. He incorporated all kinds of recycled materials into his art: bottles, glass, mirrors, cement, bathtubs, toilets, rusted bicycle frames, and cast-off jewelry. His calling as a preacher came to life at this site, where he created sermon after sermon with his art. Pursue your own sacred visions here.

84 Knox St,
Summerville, GA.
205.587.3090.
finster.com

Courtesy Paradise Gardens

Courtesy Coral Castle

Some say he had supernatural powers: Without any outside assistance or large machinery, Ed Leedskalnin single-handedly built Coral Castle. He carved and sculpted over 1100 tons of coral rock, creating a castle from the ground up using nothing but homemade tools.

The Coral Castle has numerous lookouts along the walls that were designed to help protect his privacy. In 1940, after the large carvings were in place, he finished erecting the walls, which weigh approximately 125 pounds per cubic foot. Each section of wall is eight feet tall, four feet wide, three feet thick and weighs more than 58 tons! How did he do this on his own? One wonders what the source of inspiration is that could drive a man for 28 years.

After his death, a nephew living in Michigan inherited the castle. Shortly before the nephew's death in 1953, he sold it to a family from Illinois. During the take-over, a box of Leedskalnin's personal effects was found. It contained a set of instructions that led to the discovery of 35 $100 bills—Ed Leedskalnin's life savings, earned from giving 10¢ tours in the 50's.

28655 S Dixie Hwy, Homestead, FL
(31 miles south of the Miami Airport).
305.248.6345. coralcastle.com

Panorama of Forevertron

This is not your typical sculpture park—it's better! Tom Every—70-year-old Dr Evermor—is an artist who owns a local salvage and dismantling business. He's built the world's largest scrap metal sculpture: Forevertron. At 50x120 feet, this 300-ton kinetic sculpture is assembled from relics of the industrial age—old carburetors and discarded power house machines. Construction began in 1983 and is ongoing today. Throughout the entire landscape, he has created a science-fiction space-travel-fantasy landscape with dozens of unusual-looking sculptures. You won't find Dr Evermor hanging around much anymore, but some of his artwork is still available for purchase. You can view videos of Dr Evermor at work on youtube; type "forevertron."

Thirty minutes south of Baraboo, WI, just off Hwy 12, across from the Badger Ammunitions Plant. 608.643.8009. worldofdrevermor.com

Photo ©Jon Blumb

Did you know that The Garden of Eden is actually located in a small prairie town in central Kansas? Samuel Dinsmoor, the creator of this concrete site on a quiet residential street, was a patriotic American. He started building the Garden as a residence in 1905. He opened his home as a tourist attraction three years later in 1908 and continued building until his death in 1933.

The Garden is made of limestone, cut to look like logs. A sculpture garden surrounds it. Biblical scenes mingled with political messages abound in the garden. Adam and Eve greet you as you enter the property, and Eve offers you a concrete apple. Above them on a tall, concrete tree trunk is the Devil, with frolicking children and two love storks. To the left, high in the air, a concrete Eye of God watches over garden and visitors alike. In the back yard, Labor is crucified while a banker, lawyer, preacher, and doctor nod approvingly. On one tree trunk, an octopus representing monopolies and trusts grabs at the world; a soldier and a child are trapped in two of its tentacles. On the "Goddess of Liberty" tree, Ms Liberty drives a spear through the head of an octopus as free citizens cut off the limb that it rests upon. Dinsmoor built his own 40-foot-high limestone mausoleum where he was embalmed and put on display according to his wishes—visible even today as part of the tour.

305 2nd St, Lucas, KS. 785.525.6395.
garden-of-eden-lucas-kansas.com

Photo ©Jon Blumb

Courtesy Prairie Moon Sculpture Garden

Outsider artist Herman Rusch began his garden, composed of stone, brick, concrete, glass, ceramic, shells, ferrous metals, salvaged metalwork and car parts, in 1958 and continued working on it for 16 years. Without any formal art training, he developed exceptional masonry skills. In just one year, Rusch built a 260-foot-long arched fence that spans the north perimeter of the site (above). Other sculptures include *Rocket to the Stars*, a Hindu temple, dinosaurs, and a miniature mountain. Sometimes Rusch added color to the freshly mixed concrete; sometimes he painted the surfaces. He embellished the sculptures with seashells, bits of broken bottles, and shards of crockery and mirrors. At 89 years old, he had created 40 sculptures on this site. Rusch died eleven days after celebrating his 100th birthday. His belief that "beauty creates the will to live" certainly worked in his case.

It wasn't until 1992 that the Kohler Foundation (page 72) purchased and began restoration of this site as part of its ongoing commitment to the preservation of significant art environments by self-taught artists. The conservation required structural stabilization, surface repairs, cleaning, and painting to reestablish the original palette. Landscaping revived the garden environment.

In late 1994, the Kohler Foundation donated the Prairie Moon Sculpture Garden to the Town of Milton to be maintained as a public art site.

S2921 County Rd G, Fountain City, WI. 608.687.9874. kohlerfoundation.org/rusch_bio.html

Leonard Knight at Salvation Mountain giving his trademark "thumbs up"

No need to make an appointment for this attraction! In fact, you won't be able to: Leonard Knight has no phone, electricity, or running water. Weathered by the desert, the young-spirited 80-year-old is almost always there to greet his visitors. It's as if he was expecting you when you disembark from your vehicle.

This site, located about three-miles outside Niland, pops out against the bland desert like a Fourth of July firework where this colorful masterpiece gives life to the word "naive artist."

Arriving at 11:00AM, we ducked into the caves that Knight built to stay cool; it can easily reach 105 degrees by 10AM. Wise visitors, he tells us, arrive between 5:30-9:30AM, so it is a bit cooler while they look around.

Knight has used hundreds of donated hay bales as well as over 100,000 gallons of paint to create this "man-made mountain," working mostly on his own for 20-plus years, and he doesn't appear to be slowing down. You'll find a tree made of discarded tires, a painted waterfall, crosses, hearts, and flags. If you're lucky, he'll share some of the watermelon his neighbors brought over the day before with you and you'll leave as if you were long-lost friends.

Visiting sites such as this once again prove that it is not only the art but the artist who makes the trip worthwhile. Fortunately, Leonard's land is in the process of being made into a national monument.

Knight still lives in his camper truck on the site, riding a bicycle three miles into town for supplies.

Niland, CA off highway I-8: Take Main St in downtown Niland to the east about 3 miles.

From an old postcard

This grotto was created between 1925 and 1929 by Father Mathias Wernerus with the help of the local community. It is one of the most famous of the glass, rock and cement gardens in Wisconsin.

The outside walls have six niches, each representing one of the gifts of the Holy Ghost. The rear of the structure has a relief of the Tree of Life—"The Holy Ghost Tree"—made of fossilized wood and glass.

To create the grotto, concrete was poured into slabs or modeled around metal forms and then studded with bits of glass, tiles, crockery, stone, shells, costume jewelry and other materials donated by parishioners.

In 1929-30, Father Wernerus began another shrine—"Patriotism in Stone." It is a showy and colorful tribute to Columbus, Washington, and Lincoln. There are marble statues of each man and a fountain capped with an American Eagle. Wernerus was gathering materials for another work when he got pneumonia and died in 1931.

Previously called Holy Ghost Park, this grotto was visited by 40,000 visitors a year during the 20's and 30's. Wernerus had worried that his grotto would become the biggest pilgrimage site in the country and that it would be overrun with "ice cream parlors and God knows what." But the local parish has prevented overt commercial development and it is maintained now as a county park.

→ Another well-known grotto of the 50's created by Paul M Dobberstein—Grotto of Redemption—is located in Iowa. westbendgrotto.com

305 W Main St, Dickeyville, WI (on Hwys 35 & 61, north of intersection with US 151, approx 10 miles NE of Dubuque). 608.568.7519. dickeyvillegrotto.com

Overview, Fred Smith's Wisconsin Concrete Park, Phillips, WI. Photo by Lisa Stone.

In his sixties, Fred Smith decided to channel his energy into creating sculpture. You will find over 200 pieces in the Wisconsin Concrete Park. One of Smith's earliest works was inspired by a picture of a large antlered deer jumping over a log that he had first noticed on a boy's sweater. He continued to build sculptures commemorating many events, both personal and public.

Completely self-taught in his methods of construction, using wooden armatures wrapped in wire and covered with layers of hand-mixed cement, he decorated the figures with shards of broken glass and found objects. As proprietor of the Rock Garden Tavern next door, he had a ready supply of Rhinelander Beer bottles for his sculptures. He also gladly accepted glass objects from tourists who happened by. He used everything at hand and had an innate sense of the inherent aesthetic and historical value contained in common objects.

Shortly after his death, the Kohler Foundation (page 52) purchased Fred Smith's Wisconsin Concrete Park. In February 1977, The Wisconsin Arts Board undertook the restoration of the park with funding from the National Endowment for the Arts, the State of Wisconsin, and private contributions. When restoration was completed in the fall of 1978, the Kohler Foundation gifted Wisconsin Concrete Park to Price County for use as a public art park. Friends of Fred Smith help preserve and maintain the site as a public park, an art environment, and a cultural treasure. Another big save—thank you, Kohler Foundation!

104 S Eyder St, Phillips, WI. 800.269.4505. friendsoffredsmith.org

©Exploratorium. Photo by Susan Schwartzenberg.

For residents and tourists alike, this tiny spot of land jutting into the bay allows for one of the most spectacular and serene 360-degree views of the San Francisco Bay you will ever have—and it's free! But that's not why this little gem is recommended. You can experience more than a mere view here: You can experience an environmental sculpture designed by artists Peter Richards and George Gonzales. In 1986, when they were artists-in-residence at the Exploratorium, they created this installation composed of pieces from an old Gold Rush-era cemetery and paving stones that were being moved to make way for a housing development north of San Francisco.

Periscopes pop out among the carved granite blocks. Put your ear to one of the pipes and you can hear the waves lap up against the rocks, as well as echoes of faraway places. You can sit in the "Stereo Booth," where sounds come in from three directions. It's recommended by the artists that you arrive early in the morning when the tide is high—5:30AM—as this wave-activated acoustic sculpture is at its best then and will actually sound like an organ playing in a cathedral. It's a great time to catch the sunrise too.

→ Across the street and newly renovated is The Palace of Fine Arts designed by Maynard Beck for the 1915 World Expo, which now houses one of the world's first interactive science museums—Exploratorium. You'll find lots of innovative and interesting art there, too.

San Francisco, CA. Located at the end of Yacht Rd: Park at the Yacht Club parking lot (across the street from the Exploratorium), then walk behind the Clubhouse and out onto the long jetty. exploratorium.edu/visit/wave_organ.html

Cadillac Ranch by AntFarm. Photo ©AntFarm.

As a tribute to America's "best" automobile, a collective of artists calling themselves AntFarm—Chip Lord, Hudson Marquez and Doug Michels—decided in 1974 to place 10 Cadillacs, ranging from a 1949 Club Coupe to a 1963 Sedan, in a wheat field located west of Amarillo, Texas. Stanley Marsh III, a local helium tycoon, provided a place for the cars to rest. Ten big holes were dug and the cars were driven with their front ends into the holes. In 1997, this installation was moved two miles to the west, to a cow pasture along Interstate 40, in order to place it further from the limits of the growing city. This installation has become an American icon, appearing on numerous TV shows and in many magazines and newspapers. It has been used in ads for Chrysler, Lincoln, and GE Plastics, and for products ranging from clothing and chewing gum to computers.
libertysoftware.be/cml/cadillacranch/crmain.htm

Carhenge

Jim Reinders created this installation in Alliance, Nebraska, from 38 automobiles covered in grey spray paint, as a memorial for his father. It is placed in the same proportions as Stonehenge. Additional sculptures have been erected at the site, now known as the *Car Art Reserve*.
carhenge.com

Carhenge. Photo by Kevin Saff.

Courtesy Weisman Art Museum

You guessed it! Frank Gehry is the architect. Designed in 1993, this stainless steel sculpture shines directly in your eyes as you enter the university's main campus. Its west facade reflects the setting sun as well as the water below. The large yet sparse interior galleries are lit by natural skylights.

This museum has the largest collection of Marsden Hartley paintings in the world. Other great exhibitions occur throughout the year.

The University of Minnesota also has one of the country's largest and most dynamic public art programs. Outdoor sculpture graces more than three dozen locations on the campus—building entrances, hallways, courtyards, plazas, playing fields, and even an underground mine. The artworks range from traditional sculpture to gardens to multimedia installations—some are interactive, some expressions of social and political discourse; some memorialize people and historic events. Download a map online.

Frederick R Weisman, a Minnesota native, the man for whom this museum is named, was a prolific collector.

→ You'll find another campus museum named after him in Malibu, California, at Pepperdine University (page 82).

→ You can also tour his estate in Beverly Hills (page 51) and view his private collection.

Weisman Art Museum, 333 E River Rd, Minneapolis, MN. 612.625.9494. weisman.umn.edu

Light Reign by James Turrell, 2003.
Photo by Lara Swimmer.

University of Washington

Though this space—The Henry Art Gallery—is called a gallery, it really qualifies as a museum. Known for innovative shows, it often commissions works by visually and conceptually challenging artists: Ann Hamilton, Kara Walker, Roni Horn, Jennifer Steinkamp, Tony Oursler and Maya Lin's *Systematic Landscapes*. *Light Reign*, a Skyspace (above) by James Turrell, is a permanent meditative room that combines architecture, sculpture and atmosphere. The retractable oval roof, under which you can observe the clouds and occasional black bird while sitting on the beautiful wooden seats, becomes a living painting.

Henry Art Gallery, 15th Ave NE and 41st St NE, Seattle, WA. 206.543.2281. henryart.org

---

University of Oregon

A beautiful brick building from 1933 houses the university's art collection, composed of pieces by many of today's prominent artists, both regional and national: Tobey, Graves, Archipenko, Calder, Cunningham, Diebenkorn, Hartley, Holzer, Johns, Kelly, Lawrence, Lichtenstein, Motherwell, Nauman, Neel, Moholy-Nagy, Ruscha, Kiki Smith, Gottlieb, and Viola. After renovation in 2005, the museum showed Andy Warhol's work for the grand opening. A visit in the late afternoon will mean plenty of parking, as most of the students and professors have left campus for the day.

Jordan Schnitzer Museum of Art, 1430 Johnson Ln, Eugene, OR. 541.346.3027. jsma.uoregon.edu

The historic Prince Lucien Memorial Courtyard is the heart of the Jordan Schnitzer Museum of Art.
Photo by Debbie Williamson Smith.

Nightime exterior detail of
13,000-square-foot faceted roof.
Photo by Brad Feinknopf, 2005.

The architect Rafael Viñoly has created a well-lit, multi-faceted space for visitors and students to view art. The contemporary collection, growing since the museum opened in 2005, focuses on global, emerging artists of color. The museum also houses American art including Hudson River School artists Albert Bierstadt, Jasper Cropsey and John Frederick Kensett, as well as work by Ashcan school artists John Sloan and George Wesley Bellows. The permanent collection includes works by a diverse sampling of post-1945 American artists: Christian Boltanski, William Cordova, Petah Coyne, Olafur Eiasson, David Hammons, Barkley Hendricks, Hong Lei, Paul Pfeiffer, Robin Rhode, Ed Ruscha, Kara Walker, and Eve Sussman.

Raymond Nasher, a graduate of Duke's class of 1943 with strong family ties to Duke, was one of the country's leading collectors of modern and contemporary sculpture. His estate continues to lend many works of sculpture to the museum, including the iconic Mark di Suvero sculpture *In the Bushes* on the museum's front lawn.

The travelling exhibition program focuses on modern and contemporary art and innovative, leading-edge artists. The Nasher Museum collaborates with major institutions around the world and originates exhibitions of contemporary art that travel widely.

→ See Nasher Sculpture Center in Dallas (page 28) as well as a sculpture garden in his name at the Peggy Guggenheim Collection in Venice, Italy.

Nasher Museum of Art, 2001 Campus Dr, Durham, NC. 919.684.5135. nasher.duke.edu

Beinecke Rare Book Library
This building was designed by Gordon Bunshaft—Pritzker Prize winner in 1988—of Skidmore, Owings, and Merrill. The beautiful white, gray-veined marble (alabaster) panels of the exterior are one-and-one-quarter-inch thick and are framed by light gray Vermont Woodbury granite. These marble panels filter light so that the rare materials can be displayed without damage. Take a step inside to feel the light and calm and to view the exhibits. At the entrance is Noguchi's *Sunken Court*, a zen-inspired, white marble garden.
121 Wall St, New Haven, CT. 203.432.2977.

Yale University Art Gallery
Considered Louis Kahn's most important architectural work, this building was completed while Kahn was teaching architecture at Yale. Isamu Noguchi called Kahn "a philosopher among architects." Learn more about Kahn from the video *My Architect: A Son's Journey*.

This art museum's collection comprises a rich array of paintings, drawings, prints, and sculptures by major 20th-century artists: Marisol, Giacometti, Kandisky, van Gogh's *Night Cafe*, Gaughin, Puryear, Duchamp, Ernst, Kandinsky, Léger, Mondrian, and Schwitters.
1111 Chapel St, New Haven, CT. 203.432.0600.
artgallery.yale.edu

Yale Center for British Art
Conceived by architect Louis Kahn (note the spiral staircase going up the center of the building) and finished after his death, it was the first museum in the U.S. to show a retail space in its plans.
1080 Chapel St, New Haven, CT. 203.432.2800.
yale.edu/ycba

Public art
Works of art are sited in courtyards, plazas, lobbies, and lecture halls: Claes Oldenburg's pop art icon *Lipstick (Ascending) on Caterpillar Tracks*, Maya Lin's *The Women's Table*, Roy Lichtenstein's *Modern Head*, Alexander Calder's *Gallows and Lollipops*, Richard Serra's *Stacks*, and many more. Walking tours depart from the Visitor Center, 149 Elm St. Maps online at www.yale.edu/publicart.

Ingalls Rink
Designed by Eero Saarinen in 1958 for the Yale Hockey team, and commonly called "The Whale."
73 Sachem St, New Haven, CT.

Ingalls Rink

Cantor Arts Center

An exceptional museum on an exceptional campus with a variety of great contemporary artists: Stella, Arneson, Thiebaud, Brown, Wiley, De Forest, Appel, Diebenkorn, Park, Oliviera, Wonner, Gottlieb, Hepworth, O'Keeffe, Duchamp-Villan, Lipchitz, Kupka, de Vlaminck, Rouault, Rivera, Léger, and more.

Special exhibits occur at intervals. Don't miss *Floating Peel* by Oldenburg and van Bruggen in the inner court.

Palm Dr @ Museum Wy, Palo Alto, CA. 650.723.4177. museum.stanford.edu

Stone River

Stone River is a 320-foot-long sculpture composed of 6500 stones from recycled campus buildings destroyed in the 1906 and 1989 earthquakes. Designed by Andy Goldsworthy and constructed by stonewallers from Great Britain in 2001, this serpentine earthwork lies in a trough below ground level, aligned with a tree on either end, looking somewhat like an archeological dig. You will best experience it by walking "within it" and studying and sensing the beautifully worked stones. Take your time to experience: Nature is much slower than our hectic world.

Located in front of the Cantor Arts Center under the trees. news.stanford.edu/news/2002/january23/goldsworthy-123.html

Stone River, 2001, sandstone by Andy Goldsworthy. Given in honor of Gerhard Casper, President, Stanford University, 1992-2000 by the Robert and Ruth Halperin Foundation.

Memorial Church

The Stanford Memorial Church is the physical heart of the campus, replete with stained glass windows, stunning mosaics—there are over 20,000 shades within the tiles—and stone carvings. Recently renovated due to the 1989 earthquake destruction, its smalti tiles installed by Italian artisans glisten in the California sunlight.

650.723.1762. Docent-led tour on Friday at 2PM. events.stanford.edu/events/5/563

→ *Rivers and Tides* is a fantastic documentary about Andy Goldsworthy—enthralling for adults as well as children.

Thomas Welton Stanford Art Gallery

This is a changing exhibition by professors, visiting artists, and students in a fantastic stone building.

419 Lausen Mall. art.stanford.edu/galleries-spaces/stanford-art-gallery

Photo ©Linda A Cicero, Stanford News Service

Hanna House

This house was designed by Frank Lloyd Wright in 1936 as a private residence for a young professor and his growing family. Wright used the hexagon motif as the basis for this house's layout—thus, it's sometimes called the *Honeycomb House*. It is here that Wright initiated the "grand room"—in this case, a big playroom off the kitchen where the children ruled. The walls were batten lined with aluminum foil for insulation. The concrete step waterfall, viewable from the master bedroom, used to wake the owners in the morning—an alarm set the water in motion. Though some of the central structure of the house was slightly damaged in the 1989 earthquake, not a window was broken—and there are lots of windows, as you can see from the above photo!
650.725.8352. hannahousetours.stanford.edu

Hoover Tower

Take an elevator to the top observation deck and view the campus and beyond. A carillon of 48 bells cast in Belgium rings from the top.

Public Art

Stanford University's distinguished outdoor art collection includes important figurative and abstract works in a variety of media by artists of the late 19th century to the present: Moore, Segal, Pomodoro, Miró, di Suvero, and Lin, as well as more than 70 others.
Tours available. 650.723.3469. Campus sculpture map available at the Cantor Center or online at www. museum.stanford.edu/view/outdoor_sculpture.html.

Rodin Sculpture Garden

Stanford houses the largest collection in the United States of Rodin's bronze sculpture. More than 50 works are on view inside the Cantor Center, mostly cast bronze, but also works in wax, plaster, and terra-cotta. Twenty bronzes—including *Gates of Hell,* on which Rodin worked for two decades—can be found in the Rodin Sculpture Garden. The *Burghers of Calais* are nearby on campus.
Located next to the Cantor Arts Center.
museum.stanford.edu/view/rodin_garden.html
Stuart Collection, 9500 Gilman Dr, La Jolla, CA.
858.534.2117. stuartcollection.ucsd.edu

Rodin's *Gates of Hell*

La Jolla Project, 1984 by Richard Fleischner. Stuart Collection, UC San Diego.
Photo by Phillipp Scholz Rittermann.

Site-specific sculptures commissioned by the Stuart Collection include works by Michael Asher, Jackie Ferrara, Ian Hamilton Finlay, Tim Hawkinson, Jenny Holzer, Robert Irwin, Bruce Nauman, Nam June Paik, Kiki Smith, William Wegman, and more. Wow! No wonder this campus is world-famous for its unique collection of site-specific artwork. The collection ranges from Richard Fleischner's *La Jolla Project* (above)—stone architectural forms on a sweeping green lawn, known as "Stonehenge" by students—to Elizabeth Murray's 12-foot *Red Shoe*, hidden in a eucalyptus grove. There's Alexis Smith's 560-foot-long *Snake Path* winding downhill from a terrace at Geisel Library; Niki de Saint Phalle's *Sun God* (page 128), a place of celebration for students; and Terry Allen's *Trees* (page 4), including a talking tree, a musical tree, and a silent tree. (When we stopped and hugged one of the "metal" trees, we got some strange looks from the students.) Finding these sculptures on this large campus, even with a map, is somewhat like a scavenger hunt with great prizes. Visiting all these wonderful sculptures at the beautiful 1200-acre campus with its chaparral-filled canyons and eucalyptus groves made me want to go back to school—here!

Don't miss the amazing architecture of Geisel Library—a fantastic "spaceship" by William Pereira, 1960, expanded in 1993 by Gunnar Birkerts (page 3). Within this building is the work of John Baldessari.

.

9500 Gilman Dr, La Jolla, CA. 858.534.2117. Download a map and detailed information about the sculptures: stuartcollection.ucsd.edu.

Foreground sculpture by Hans Van de Bovenkamp; background by Philip Grausman. Photo ©Bob Handelman.

The largest outdoor sculpture park in Brooklyn stretches across Pratt Institute's 25-acre campus. With rotating exhibits, it has featured sculptors such as Serra, Lipski, di Suvero, Indiana, and many more. The park was recognized as one of the 10 best college and university campus art collections in the country by *Public Art Review* in 2006. Visitors can also view exhibitions at The Rubelle and Norman Schafler Gallery on this campus and at Pratt Manhattan Gallery, the Institute's Manhattan campus—144 W 14th St, 2nd Floor.
200 Willoughby Ave, Brooklyn, NY. 718.636.3600.
pratt.edu/about_pratt/visiting_pratt/tour_the_campus/sculpture_park

---

Pepperdine University
This university museum rotates exhibits of contemporary art by professional artists every three months, focusing on the recent art of California. Though the exhibition space is small—3000 square feet—the presentation is more than satisfying. Past exhibitions have featured

internationally acclaimed artists such as Dale Chihuly, Jim Dine, and Wayne Thiebaud. The museum had an exhibition of over 60 original works by Roy Lichtenstein in 2011. Don't miss the awesome view of the Pacific Ocean, too!
Frederick R Weisman Museum of Art, 24255 Pacific Coast Hwy, Malibu, CA. 310.506.4851.
arts.pepperdine.edu/museum

Courtesy Pepperdine University

Photo courtesy Arizona State University Art Museum

Nelson Fine Arts Center

The changing exhibitions in this three-floor museum—49,700 square feet with five galleries—feature paintings, sculpture, drawing, ceramics, and more. Included is work by Karel Appel, Deborah Butterfield, William T Wiley, Kim Abeles, and Xu Bing among others. *Art in America* calls it "the single most impressive venue in Arizona for contemporary art." The Ceramics Research Center, within the museum, houses an outstanding collection of ceramics from Latin America and Cuba.

10th & Mill Ave, Tempe, AZ. 480.965.2787. asuartmuseum.asu.edu

Grady Gammage Memorial Auditorium

Constructed in 1962, this is the last major nonresidential building that Frank Lloyd Wright designed (adapted from one of his unbuilt projects for an opera house in Baghdad). The circular structure's long, elegant pedestrian ramps connecting to the parking areas are more decorative than practical. Inside, the aisle spacing is most generous, even with 3000 seats. Acoustically, it is said to be one of the best auditoriums in the country. Artwork is exhibited throughout the year on the main floor in the David Scoular Galleries.

1200 S Forest Ave, Tempe, AZ. 480.965.0458. asu.edu/tour/main/ggma.html

Public art

This 700-acre campus with 65,000 students—the largest in the nation—could easily take you an entire day to explore all the art, from Depression-era murals to contemporary sculpture. It was named to the "Top Ten" of campus public art programs by *Sculpture Magazine*. Download a map online at www.herbergercollege.asu.edu/public_art.

College of Law

The artwork throughout the halls has a Southwestern flair.

Armstrong Hall, Orange St & McAllister Ave.

Gallery 100

Exhibitions of graduating-art majors are held here.

Engineering Building A, Room ECA 100

BAMscape. Courtesy of BAM/PFA. Photo by Marion Brenner.

Architect Mario Ciampi of San Francisco won the 1964 design competition for this museum creation—a distinct modernist design with many levels and angles in the interior and a most interesting architectural piece. This well-respected space hangs avant-garde exhibits in its minimal environment. The spaciousness of each gallery allows each artwork to have its own aura revealed. Never a dull moment here: Eva Hesse, Kurt Schwitters, Juan Gris, Jay DeFeo, Robert Colescott, Joan Brown, Robert Mapplethorpe, Sebastião Salgado, Paul Kos, James Castle, and many others have had exhibits. In 1970, artist and professor Hans Hofmann donated 45 paintings and $250,000 to the university.

→ A walk on the serene UC campus will take you to sculpture by Calder, Benton, Stackpole, Hunt, Pomodoro, Jerome Kirk, and more.

→ Across the street (south of the tennis courts) is Hearst Memorial Gymnasium, designed by Maynard Beck and Julia Morgan. Take a walk up to the second floor to see the beautiful swimming pool area.

→ If you need a place to rest your head for the night, The Berkeley Club is only a few blocks away (2315 Durant Ave). Designed in 1929 by Julia Morgan—architect of Hearst Castle, who called this her "little castle"—this Romanesque and Moorish-style building is now a California Historical Landmark. The interior spaces and the indoor swimming pool exude old-world charm. You'll have a lovely view of the San Francisco Bay or the Berkeley hills.

Berkeley Art Museum, 2626 Bancroft Wy, Berkeley, CA. 510.642.0808. bampfa.berkeley.edu

Architect: The Freelon Group. Photo by James West, JWestProductions.com

The Turchin Center for the Visual Arts (TCVA) is located on the campus of Appalachian State University and provides visitors with a dynamic year-round program, rotating 20-25 exhibits each year. Exhibitions focus on a blend of new, contemporary works as well as historically important artwork. The center features nationally and internationally renowned artists—Robert Motherwell, Tim Turner, Andy Warhol, Hiroshi Yamano—as well as many of the finest artists in the region. Multi-faceted programs are offered at the center, including lectures, workshops, and other special events.

The pedestrian gateway outside the center—featuring several areas for public sculpture, including the Kay Borkowski Sculpture Garden—connects the community area to the campus.

The Rosen Outdoor Sculpture Competition & Exhibition is a national juried competition presented annually by the Turchin Center. Ten sculptures are selected by a juror—specifically chosen and different each year—for a 10-month exhibition, May through February, and are placed in public outdoor settings across the campus. The "Sculpture Walk" in July is an opportunity for visitors to walk and talk with the juror who decided on the 10 winners—to discover more from the juror's point of view.

Turchin Center for Visual Arts, 423 W King St, Boone, NC. 828.262.3017. turchincenter.org

View of the UCLA Franklin D Murphy Sculpture Garden with Gerhard Marcks's *Maja*, 1941. Photo ©Joshua White.

The Franklin D Murphy Sculpture Garden
The 70 sculptures at UCLA span over five acres on campus: Arp, Butterfield, Calder, Hepworth, Lipchitz, Marcks, Moore, Falkenstein, Rodin's *The Walking Man*, David Smith, and more. Los Angeles, CA. hammer.ucla.edu/collections

Eli and Edythe Broad Art Center
Designed by Richard Meier—recipient of the 1984 Pritzker Prize—this center is an excellent site where residents of Los Angeles as well as visitors can view art. It exhibits artwork from faculty, undergraduates, and MFA students from around the world. The plaza in front features Richard Serra's enormous T.E.U.C.L.A., a 42.5-ton torqued ellipse. Los Angeles, CA. arts.ucla.edu/BroadArtCenter.htm

Hammer Museum
This off-campus facility is one of the foremost university art museums in the country. The Hammer's collections and exhibitions span the classic to the contemporary in art, with a special emphasis on new work created in the last 10 years. Particular attention is paid to works by artists from Southern California. The museum has a reputation for exhibitions that shed light on lesser-known artists, whether they are young and emerging or simply overlooked by history. The permanent collection has an emphasis on Old Masters, French Impressionists, and Post-Impressionists: Rembrandt, Goya, van Gogh, Degas, Corot, Fragonard, Moreau, Cassatt, Rubens, Singer Sargent, and Titian. 10899 Wilshire Blvd, Los Angeles, CA. 310.443.7000. hammer.ucla.edu

Hammer Exterior.
Photo ©Elon Schoenholz.

Public Art

Over the the years, the campus at MIT has become a museum, with works of art sited indoors and out throughout the acreage: Calder, Bartlett, Heizer, Nevelson, Moore, Tony Smith, Picasso, Pepper, Olitski, di Suvero's *Aesop's Fables II*. The fun architecture of the Frank Gehry-designed Ray & Maria Strata Center can best be viewed from the quad area (below). Sarah Sze's *Blue Poles* can be found on the side of Sidney-Pacific Graduate Residence Hall. In the Physics and Engineering Building is *Bars of Color with Squares*, a terrazzo floor comprised of 15 boldly colored sections of geometric patterns by Sol LeWitt (right). One of my favorite pieces is Frank Stella's *Loohooloo*, located in the conference room of the Rogers Building. It wraps around the

Sol LeWitt, *Bars of Color within Squares*, (MIT), 2007. Photo by George Bouret.

entire room for 100 feet, undulating with exciting strokes and colors. (You'll have to ask an attendant to unlock the room for you.)

Don't miss the cylindrical chapel designed by Eero Saarinen. (He also designed Kresge Auditorium next door.) The chapel's centerpiece is dramatized by a shimmering golden altar designed by sculptor Harry Bertoia. Download an art map online.

List Visual Arts Center

The Weisner Building that houses the List Visual Arts Center was designed by I M Pei. The center focuses on exhibiting contemporary art. With five changing exhibits annually, the List explores challenging and intellectually inquisitive contemporary art.

Each year a lottery is held for students. Over 300 works of art, primarily prints and photographs, are loaned to students through the highly popular Student Loan Art Program.

20 Ames St, BldgE15,
Cambridge, MA.
617.253.4680.
Check for summer hours.
listart.mit.edu

Ray & Maria Strata Center.
Frank Gehry architect.

Frost Art Museum

This 46,000-square-foot facility was designed in 2008 by internationally recognized architect Yann Weymouth, who also designed the new Dali Museum in Florida (page 47). The structure features a soaring three-story glass atrium entrance and a dramatically suspended staircase leading to the second and third floors. Natural daylight permeates most of the galleries. Contemporary artwork is shown. Three of the nine galleries are dedicated to the permanent collection, while the remaining six galleries feature temporary exhibitions. Included in the permanent collection is The Betty Laird Perry Emerging Artist Collection.

11200 SW 8th St, Miami, FL. 305.348.2890. thefrost.fiu.edu

Argosy by Alexander Liberman, 1980. Painted steel, 363x228x144". University Collection, Florida International University, Miami, Florida. Gift of Martin Z Marguilies Family Collection, UC 2008.9.

The Sculpture Park at FIU

This sculpture park displays over 70 artworks in a variety of media throughout the 26-acre subtropical landscape. It is recognized nationally as one of the most important collections of sculpture and the largest on a university campus. Comprised of gifts and loans from private donors and purchases through the Florida Art in State Purchasing Program, the sculpture park features works by such celebrated artists as Steve Tobin, Jacques Lipchitz, Anthony Caro, Jean Claude Rigaud, Charles Ginnever and many others.

SW 107 Ave & SW 16 St. www2.fiu.edu/~mzmpark

The Creative Growth Art Center provides a stimulating environment for artistic instruction to physically, mentally, and developmentally disabled adult artists. The on-site gallery that sells artwork created by the artists working at Creative Growth has gained a stellar reputation—lines are wrapped around the block for openings. Judith Scott started a highly acclaimed career as a yarn-and-string artist while working here. Dwight Macintosh is also gaining world recognition. If you have a particular item or artist in mind, you had better get to the opening early—work sells fast! Better yet, stop by any weekday during gallery hours and shop, or have a tour of the workshop area where artists are busy creating. Great prices and fun artwork—you'll get addicted to this innovative venue.

→ Similar venues across the country with galleries selling art:

New York City: hainyc.org
Grass Valley, CA: neighborhoodcenterofthearts.org
Richmond, CA: niadart.org
San Francisco, CA: creativityexplored.org
El Cajon, CA: stmsc.org
Washington, DC: art-enables.org;
   vsadc.org; vsarts.org
Minneapolis, MN: interactcenter.com
Albuquerque, NM: vsartsnm.org
Philadelphia, PA: nuvisionsart.com
Seattle, WA: thevisiongallery.org

355 24th St, Oakland, CA. 510.836.2340. www.creativegrowth.org

Staircase at Torpedo Factory Art Center. Photo by Jim Steele.

Thirty years in the making, the Torpedo Factory Art Center is one of the first experiments whereby a group of artists decided to take an old building and remodel it for studio space with their own manpower and money. This waterfront venue—a former torpedo plant—was transformed into a beautiful and popular showcase for the arts. Over 160 artists work and sell their wares on the premises: painters, sculptors, jewelers, fiber artists and more. Special events as well as educational opportunities take place through The Art League School year-round, attracting over 500,000 visitors annually. You can observe artists creating in any of the 82 studio spaces at almost any hour of the day. Artists treat their spaces like a professional gallery,

exhibiting and selling their work (with prices marked) directly from their studios. Some of the current artists, and many in the past, have worked hard to make this art center one of the most enjoyable I've seen in my travels. Details make a difference here: Heavy metal double-doors painted in cheery colors of pink, turquoise, orange, and red (with matching stairs), as well as huge glass windows, are just two of the features that energize what could easily be a dull, dark space.

Be sure to ascend the great stairway leading to the second floor (above). Plan to spend a couple hours browsing all three floors and chatting with the working artists. The entire first floor is dedicated to art-related sales venues.

105 N Union St, Alexandria, VA. 703.838.4565. torpedofactory.org

Artwork by Mri Pilar. Photo by Steven Schultz. Courtesy Grassroots Art Center.

The Grassroots Art Center opened in 1995 and occupies three turn-of-the-century native limestone buildings. Located in a town of only 500 people, this museum is not the only art-related attraction in town. An all-day plan is recommended in order to digest the visual feast in this town: Deeble Rock Garden, Garden of Isis, Trash Art Workshop, Flying Pig Gallery, World's Largest Collection of the World's Smallest Versions of the World's Largest Things Traveling Museum and Roadside Attraction, G-wiz Garage, Snow Dome House, Garden of Eden (page 68), and more. An online map can be downloaded with more information about each venue. Grassroots art is made by people with no formal artistic training, sometimes referred to as visionary, art brut, primitive, intuitive, or outsider art. Often, artists create an entire environment. Kansas ranks third in the number of such environments, following California in first place and Wisconsin in second.

213 S Main St, Lucas, KS. 785.525.6118. grassrootsart.net

Artwork by Bill Winsdor. Photograph by Roslyn Schultz. Courtesy Grassroots Art Center.

Courtesy Bemis Center for Contemporary Arts

In 1981, artist Jun Kaneko, a well-known ceramicist, along with Tony Hepburn, Lorne Falke, and Ree Schonlau, founded the Bemis Center for Contemporary Arts. Their edict was that exceptional talent deserves to be supported. Bemis began providing well-equipped studio space, living accommodations, and a monthly stipend to artists-in-residence. These artists come from around the world to work within a supportive community of like-minded people.

The atmosphere and environment at Bemis offer an ideal situation for creative growth and experimentation, encouraging artists to confront artistic challenges. Emphasis is placed on a collaborative atmosphere conducive to self-challenge and experimentation. Past residents have included Neri, Nash, Watanabe, Aycock, and more.

The Bemis Center presents 10-12 cutting-edge exhibitions annually. These shows, which run in the Center's three main galleries, feature emerging and established artists and span all the visual media including video, installation, and performance.

A full-hour tour offers an enriching experience for the visitor: A staff member guides you through all three galleries, discussing current exhibitions and programs, then to the second floor to meet two artists-in-residence in their studios and hear brief descriptions of their work. An annual auction occurs in late fall.

724 S 12th St, Omaha, NE. 402.341.7130.

Courtesy Bemis Center for Contemporary Arts

Fallingwater, Courtesy of Western Pennsylvania Conservancy

Even before his birth, Frank Lloyd Wright's mother deemed him an architect. As a child, he was encouraged to play with Froebel's system of toys, which consisted mostly of cubes, cylinders, and squares—shaped objects in deep primary colors. At age 21, he signed a five-year contract with the firm of Adler & Sullivan, the most prominent firm in Chicago at the time. He proved to be too independent to stay any longer than his contract, so in 1895 he built his own studio adjacent to his Oak Park, Chicago, home (which you can now tour: darwinmartinhouse.org). His career and private life had radical ups and downs. Considered the greatest of modern architects, his innovative school of architecture still functions today with two locations (page 96).

Fallingwater

Possibly the best-known private house in the world, Fallingwater is an international architectural landmark just 45 minutes from Pittsburgh. It is one of the best of Wright's examples of integrating nature into the home, with the cantilevered terraces stretching over the stream, making "white sound" predominant. Built between 1936-1939, it is the only Wright house open to the public with original furnishings and artwork intact.

1491 Mill Run Rd, Mill Run, PA. 724.329.8501. fallingwater.org

Kentuck Knob

Near to Fallingwater is Wright's Usonian-style house built in 1956. A meadow exhibiting 35 sculptures by Goldsworthy, Ray Smith, Caro, and others is situated below the house.

723 Kentuck Rd, Chalk Hill, PA. 724.329.1901. kentuckknob.com

Interior view. Photo by John F Hughes.

Marin County Civic Center

Both a National and State Historic Landmark, this public building was designed by Frank Lloyd Wright in 1957 at age 90. One of his last—#770—and one of his most distinctive designs, he did not live to see it completed. Wright said "I'll bridge these hills with graceful arches"—and so he did: The arch and circle theme are used throughout the building. The Civic Center, which houses Marin County's administrative offices, county court rooms, and jail, spans three hills. Its sculptural sky-blue roof, scalloped balconies, and golden spire are so extraordinary that it was the location for the 1997 science fiction movie *Gattica*. The main gate has elaborate grillwork with golden circles and arches. Don't miss the first-floor model of the original architectural plan for the entire complex (some of which was not constructed).

The second-floor cafe—where you'll meet if you go on the tour—has a fantastic view of eastern Marin, as well as a hidden patio with a tiny pond. You can wander around the entire center at your own leisure, if you prefer. You'll find art exhibits on the first and third floors that add to the aesthetic harmony of the interior. The skylights over the mall were not part of the original design but were added later for protection from the weather. Wright used sheep's wool with acoustical paint on the dome of the library to keep it quieter.

3501 Civic Center Dr, San Rafael, CA. 415.499.7009. co.marin.ca.us

Spire

S C Johnson Administration Building and Research Tower
The lighting in this rather enclosed building, and its principal supports—mushroom-shaped columns—made this building a new model for its time in 1936. The employees loved the starkness and natural light. Wright also designed all the office furniture for the building, most in metal. Various hour-long tours are available; reservations are required well in advance. Plan your day so you can stay for an informative film before or following your tour.
1525 Howe St, Racine, WI. 262.260.2154. racinecounty.com/golden/wright.htm

V C Morris
This is one of my favorite buildings designed by Frank Lloyd Wright. The arched entrance of brick seems to go unnoticed on this busy alley. Entering the building, presently occupied by Xanadu Gallery, you see an elegant spiral staircase, reminiscent of the Guggenheim Museum in New York City. The store occupants are welcoming and allow anyone to look around. My favorite part was a concrete domed ceiling directly above the sales counter that was painted in a pastel abstract. This building is so inspiring that I try to stop in every time I am in the heart of San Francisco.
140 Maiden Ln, San Francisco, CA. 415.392.9999. xanadugallery.us

Spring Green. Photo by Judith Bromley.

Taliesin Spring Green

This is a spectacular 600-acre estate located approximately 40 miles from Madison, named after a Welsh poet and literally meaning "shining brow." Spring Green was the valley where Wright's Welsh ancestors settled in the 1800's. In 1904, Wright's mother purchased the sprawling land upon which he built a 37,000-square-foot complex that grew to include living quarters, guest rooms, apartments, a drafting studio and office, a complete working farm, orchards, berry patches, vineyards, kitchen gardens, and a hydro-electric plant. Wright also began teaching students at this location. In 1976, it was designated a National Historic Landmark. A variety of tours are available.

5481 County Highway C, Spring Green, WI. 608.588.2511. taliesinpreservation.org

Taliesin West

Wright's desert school in the Scottsdale suburbs, outside of Phoenix, was his western headquarters. It is still used today as a teaching facility, as well as living space for teachers and

Taliesen West. Photo by Judith Bromley.

students. Wright believed that architects should experience the building process firsthand, so his students did just that (and still do). Wright and his students used the rocks and sand of the desert to create buildings appropriate to the site. A variety of tours are available.

12621 N Frank Lloyd Wright Blvd, Scottsdale, AZ. 480.860.2700 franklloydwright.org

Arcosanti Vaults, viewed from north. This large public area provides space for events and meetings. Photo by Yuki Yanagimoto.

Based on the concept of arcology—architecture plus ecology—Arcosanti is Paolo Soleri's model for how the world will build cities in the future. Under construction since 1970, upon completion it will house over 5000 pioneers. Construction is slow because residents and workshop attendees—over 7000 alumni since 1970—create the labor force. Funds are raised by special events, workshops, donations, and sales of wind chimes constructed on the "campus." The general tour is a must to understand Soleri's concepts and ideas. You will view his drawings—futuristic and beautiful. Try to stay for a meal. (We ended up staying for three.) The food is delicious—or is it the open air that tastes so good? Seeing Arcosanti without staying the night would be missing 50 percent of its charm. The overnight facilities are clean, quiet, simple, and inexpensive. The magnificent view of the far-reaching western lands and the solitude at night are a far cry from the big city. Stay longer to take walks and explore the environment or take a one-day silt casting workshop on select days of the month—only $20 and it includes a tour. Citizens from around the world can take a more extensive workshop (five weeks) to learn more.

→ When in Scottsdale, don't miss the *Soleri Pedestrian Bridge* that spans the Arizona Canal at Scottsdale's waterfront, southwest of Scottsdale and Camelback Roads.

Arconsanti, Cordes Junction, AZ. 928.632.7135. arcosanti.org

Arcosanti, southern exposure. Photo by Chris Ohlinger.

Disney Concert Hall

The Disney Concert Hall is an outstanding example of Frank Gehry's—awarded the Pritzker Prize in 1989—innovative work.

As a boy, he played with blocks and scraps of wood his grandmother recycled from a fix-it shop, creating cities and structures, much like he does today as he works on a project. His innovative character was keynoted by Apple computer in their "Think Different" campaign.

Though he grew up in Canada, his family moved to Los Angeles, where he eventually went to USC. Starting in the art department, he soon switched to architecture. A palm reader told him as a young child, though it didn't mean much to him then, that he was going to be a great architect some day.

He has also designed and successfully sold furniture and lamps. Knowing this would ultimately be a deviation from his main interest—architecture—he left his inventions behind, even though they were profitable. At heart, he is a sculptor and readily admits that he envies painters. A few pieces of his sculpture are exhibited around the world: A glass fish—each of its scales a separate piece of glass—sits inside an outdoor pavilion at the Walker Museum in Minneapolis; *Monumental Fish*, made of bronze-colored stainless steel (left) sits high above the boardwalk in Barcelona at Hotel Artes.

A video about Gehry, *Sketches of Frank Gehry*, by Sidney Pollack is a great watch.

A self-guided or guided tour of the hall can be taken on most days of the week.

Disney Concert Hall, 111 S Grand Ave, Los Angeles, CA. 323.850.2000. musiccenter.org

Photo courtesy of The Seattle Public Library

Designed by avant-garde Dutch architect Rem Koolhaas—sometimes called Cool House—this 2004 diamond-shaped creation is an amazing addition to Seattle's skyline—a library that actually attracts tourists! Koolhaas won the Pritzker Prize in 2000 and was lauded for "bold, strident, thought-provoking architecture." Indeed it is. His designs are also known for their economy per square foot and their combination of materials.

The fourth floor of this library, where meeting rooms are housed, is entirely red, and I mean deep, blood red. The energy is electric. When you walk into the bathroom, however, you will find calming baby blue. Your kids will love the yellow elevators, which extend three floors, where you will encounter *Talking Heads* by Tony Oursler (below). The carved maple floor by Ann Hamilton has 556 lines of raised text in 11 languages, with reversed type. The 10th floor allows you to read in natural light as well as see downtown Seattle and Elliott Bay. Video-projection artist Gary Hill has a 40-foot-square artwork on the white atrium wall, best viewed from this level.

With all these artistic surprises popping up, it's no wonder this spot is pleasantly humming with hundreds of busy computer terminals and lots of intellectual and visual delights.

The Seattle Public Library, 1000 4th Ave, Seattle, WA. 206.386.4636. spl.org

Talking Heads by Tony Oursler. Photo courtesy of The Seattle Public Library.

The Sundial Bridge

Designed by world-renowned Spanish architect Santiago Calatrava, the Sundial Bridge is the calling card for this small town in Northern California. At a cost of $12 million, it's Calatrava's first bridge in the United States, spanning 700 feet across the Sacramento River. It is suspended by cables anchored to a 217-foot-high pylon, hovering above a salmon-spawning area within the Turtle Bay Exploration Park. A walking-only bridge, the stunning pale-blue glass walkway evokes a sense of weightlessness. The all-white steel and mosaic surfaces create a stunning work of art. Seen from Highway 101 as you drive north, it's a huge structure spanning high above the trees. Only two miles off the freeway, it is a must-walk-on adventure.

→ Calatrava also designed the Milwaukee Art Museum.

→ View *The Wave* in Dallas, Texas, at Southern Methodist University. The entryway of the Meadows Museum is where you'll find his first large-scale kinetic sculpture—26x68 feet—featuring perpetually-moving, hollow-steel, bronze-coated bars that rise and descend in a syncopation that simulates a wave motion. meadowsmuseumdallas.org

→ His web site, www.calatrava.com, is an art piece in itself. Be sure to view his New York City Ballet stage design online.

Sundial Bridge, Turtle Bay Exploration Park, Redding, CA. 800.887.8532. turtlebay.org

Defenestration by Brian Goggin. Photo by Brian Goggin.

Defenestration literally means "to throw out the window." That's exactly what this artist—Brian Goggin—has done with the help of 100 volunteers: Desks, light fixtures, sofas, chairs, tables, clocks, refrigerators, and more have been tossed out the windows. This "sculptural mural" appears to have the furniture crawling on the building. All the pieces are recycled: Who'd want to hang a new refrigerator out an abandoned building? View more of his work online. You'll see what fun he has with recycled items, such as the old suitcases in the picture below.

214 6th St @ Howard St, San Francisco, CA.
metaphorm.org

Sampson by Brian Goggin
Sacramento, California Airport
Photo by Brian Goggin

Photo by Eirik Johnson

Philip Johnson—1979 Pritzker Prize winner—designed his house on 47 acres in 1949, bequeathing it to the nation in 1986. With no actual rooms—only objects acting as dividers—the 1792-square-foot room seems immense.

The Painting Gallery, one of the 14 structures on the grounds, was designed to house his collection of modern paintings—Salle, Stella, Rauschenberg, Schnabel, Warhol, Schulman, and Sherman. Inspiration came from a tomb in Mycanae, Greece: Entry is via a grass-covered mound.

For his sculpture collection, Johnson designed another structure, also inspired by the Greek islands, with a series of squares at 45 degrees to each other. The five-level interior with many staircases was his impression of Greece: "Every street is a staircase to somewhere." You will find sculptural works by Heizer, Rauschenberg, Chamberlain, Segal, Stella, Nauman, Morris, and more.

A variety of tours are available.

→ Glass and steel construction had become commonplace by 1960, and Johnson began designing crystal-type structures sheathed in glass. He joined Mies van der Rohe for the design of the 39-story Seagram Building in New York in 1956 as well as the Four Seasons Restaurant. In 1967, he designed the Kreeger Museum (page 53), the Art Museum of South Texas, and the Crystal Cathedral in California.

→ Johnson donated nearly 2000 pieces of art to MOMA.

Glass House, New Canaan, CT. 202.594.9884. philipjohnsonglasshouse.org

Photo by Whit Slemmons.

E Fay Jones, AIA Gold Medal winner in 1990 and once an apprentice to Frank Lloyd Wright and a professor at the University of Arkansas at Fayetteville, designed this chapel in the late 70's.

Nestled in a woodland setting, Thorncrown Chapel rises 48 feet into the Ozark sky. This magnificent wooden structure contains 425 windows and over 6000 square feet of glass. It sits atop 100 tons of native flagstone. The chapel's simple design and majestic beauty combine to make it what critics have called "one of the finest religious spaces of modern times."

Thorncrown Chapel was selected as the fourth most favored building in a poll of the membership of the American Institute of Architects!

Thorncrown was the dream of Jim Reed, a native of Pine Bluff, Arkansas. In 1971, Jim purchased the land—now the site of the chapel—to build his retirement home. People admired his choice of location and would often stop at his property to gain a better view of the beautiful Ozark hills. Instead of fencing them out, Jim decided to invite them in. One day, while walking up the hill to his house, he and his wife got the idea to build a chapel in the woods to give wayfarers an inspiring place to relax. On March 23, 1979, the construction crew broke ground on the mountainside. Jim's dream would soon be a reality. The chapel opened in 1980. Over 5,000,000 people have visited this woodland sanctuary!

→ Other buildings by E Faye Jones include residences as well as chapels: the well-kown Mildred B Cooper Memorial Chapel in Bella Vista, Arkansas is the best example.

12968 Hwy 62 West, Eureka Springs, AR. 479.253.7401. thorncrown.com

Photo by Rich Villacorta

Designed by 1996 Pritzker Prize-winning architect Jose Rafael Moneo of Spain, this structure was finished in 2002. (The former church was demolished in the Los Angeles earthquake of 1994.) Created at a cost of $189 million, it includes $6 million of artwork by nine southern-California artists.

A worthwhile guide to the vast amount of art in the cathedral can be acquired at a kiosk on the church grounds. It includes such interesting facts as: There are 60,000 paving stones in a circular pattern centered at the altar; the tallest of the pipes in the organ is 40 feet high; nearly 12,000 panes of translucent, veined alabaster are used in place of the more traditional stained glass. Robert Graham designed the 25-ton set of 30-foot-high bronze doors.

Lita Albuquerque created a water wall and fountain in the plaza. A water court—a multilevel plaza landscaped with fountains— has waterfalls and trellises and is used for concerts.

This massive church with angular walls is able to seat 3000-4500 people. Be sure to walk in the ambulatories; if you happen to visit during a rehearsal, the music and voices from the side aisles are exquisite, and the organ is massive and powerful.

Walk to the crypt mausoleum below the main cathedral. You will find total silence. Beautiful stained glass windows are the only element besides the vast amount of marble.

A most impressive modern church, it creates the same awe as Chartres Cathedral.

555 W Temple St, Los Angeles, CA. 213.680.5200. olacathedral.org

Interior view of Quaker Meeting Hall; Skyspace at top

In a simple Houston suburb is where this Skyspace—a 12-foot square opening in the meeting house's barrel-like ceiling—is located. It was designed by James Turrell, who is sometimes referred to as the "Artist of Light."

On most Friday evenings when the Live Oak Friends Meeting occurs, approximately 20 minutes before sunset, you can sit for an hour of meditation and view the Skyspace as the sun sets and transforms the sky into an intensely blue "canvas." At first, clouds and birds bring perspective through the Skyspace and remind viewers that this is "live." As it gets darker, the canvas—the sky—appears to lower into the room. The effect is mesmerizing; you will feel like you can reach out and touch the color blue and hold it in your hands. At one point when I attended and no clouds were present, it looked like a Day-Glo fluorescent light in the ceiling. When the clouds go away and only a blue sky remains, visions start getting blurred. Depth perception becomes lost after viewing for a period of time, as it becomes very black. The roof remains open approximately 40 minutes after sunset. The Skyspace is then closed, the "painting" disappears, and you walk out a different person.

→ The Roden Crater, a dormant volcano, is also being developed by Turrell outside of Flagstaff, Arizona, in the Painted Desert. His most ambitious project, the concept began in 1972, with major construction finally beginning in 1999. In the works to this day, it presently does not have an opening date scheduled. Keep it on your list of future sites to visit.

→ See Henry Art Gallery (page 76).

Live Oak Friends Meetinghouse, 1318 W 26th St, Houston, TX. 713.862-6685. Check online to see what time the sun is setting on the evening you want to attend. friendshouston.org/skyspace.html

Double Negative

Double Negative is considered the first "earthwork." In 1969, Michael Heizer, a pioneer in earthworks, dynamited and bulldozed this monument. Inspired by Egyptian ruins—1500 foot long, 30 foot wide, five stories high, displacing 40,000-200,000 tons, costing $30,000 ($150,000 today)—this creation rises out of a mesa overlooking the Virgin River, 70 miles northeast of Las Vegas.

As you ascend onto the mesa, you will most likely be all alone—an introspective experience. When you arrive at this earthwork, you will see boulders tumbling into the interior from 35 years of weathering. You can still walk down into the negative space and experience the silence. It took me awhile to figure out where the title *Double Negative* came from. I almost missed the reflected gully across the far mesa, a duplicate of the one I was standing in. If you like exploring, you'll have a blast on this adventure.

Overton, NV. doublenegative.tarasen.net For directions: arttravelguide.info/doublenegative

Lightning Field

Created by American sculptor Walter De Maria, *Lightning Field* was installed in 1977. Known as a work of "land art," it is located in the remote high desert in southwestern New Mexico. It is comprised of 400 polished stainless steel poles installed in a grid—one mile by one kilometer. At an elevation of 7200 feet, the summer months are mild; however, storms do arise and evenings can be chilly. Thunderstorms occur about 60 days of the year, chances are one in five that your visit will produce lightning on the rods.

A visit to this installation includes dinner, overnight, and breakfast—a complete experience, to say the least. When you arrive at the remote pick-up location, you will be told nothing about anything—and I will tell you no more than we were told! It is, thus, a very personal and mysterious experience. Reservations are needed well in advance.

New Mexico. 505.898.3335. diacenter.org lightningfield@msn.com kshields1@earthlink.com

Courtesy Museum of Glass

Inside the Museum of Glass you will find a vast cavern—the Hot Shop—where you can watch glass artists at work on their medium. Changing exhibitions occur inside this 75,000-square-foot museum designed by Canadian architect Arthur Erickson, which includes a now-iconic tilted cone (above).

Outside is a 500-foot span of walkway—Chihuly's *Bridge of Glass*—that includes two Crystal Towers and a Venetian Wall (above). Glorius colors radiate on both sides as you walk across the bridge.

No one will dispute that the master artist of glass in America is Dale Chihuly. Tacoma, where he grew up, has honored him with this museum dedicated to glass. Many of his art pieces are also located around town. Steps away from this museum, at Union Station, you will find five installations that hang beneath the 90-foot dome of this historic landmark. When you view some of his work, you will know why he is "The Man."

→ With the help of Anne Gould and John Hauberg, Chihuly founded Pilchuck Glass School (www.pilchuck.com) in 1971. It is open to the public only one Sunday per year for touring—a fundraiser for the school.

→ Attend the annual Black-Tie Auction (October in Seattle) where you can bid on well-known, emerging, and student glass work.

→ *Chichuly: Gardens and Glass* is a book about his magnificent installation in Chicago Gardens.

→ Chihuly's website has wonderful videos you can view about him and his assistants creating work. A variety of videos on Chihuly's work are also available from Netflix.

Museum of Glass, 1801 E Dock St, Tacoma, WA. 253.396.1768. Ear for Art at 888.411.4220: recorded information about glass art around Tacoma. museumofglass.org

Exhibition in beehive kiln. Courtesy Feats of Clay.

This event is our winner for the "Most Unique Exhibit Opening." The opening occurs annually in April. It is held in a stadium-size ceramic factory, where you are immediately taken aback by the loud roaring: Several bee-hive kilns are heating, readying themselves for baking. Part of the exhibit is installed in one of the unused beehive kilns (above). Entering this unique kiln was similar to entering a small Egyptian tomb, full of mystery and awe. About 30 of the winning-entry pieces from the annual competition—78 or so pieces in all—are displayed in two circular rows around the room. When we visited, the second part of the exhibit was held on the third floor in another part of the factory. The 15x30-foot elevator is 125 years old—the oldest this side of the Missouri, we were told. Arriving in a hollow-sounding area filled with drumming invoked a rather mystical feeling.

The exhibit was set amidst the rubble of terra-cotta "beings" in a dusty, mysterious, and remote part of the factory. Wine, drummers, dimmed lighting, and a huge cavern created the inviting background. The artwork was marvelous. Unfortunately, most of the pieces had already been purchased earlier that evening by experienced attendees; these attendees knew which special tickets to buy, allowing them to enter the exhibition at its earliest opening and thus have first choice to some of the best-priced ceramic pieces I've seen. The show continues through the end of May.

→ Other ceramic shows: Ceramics Showcase, Portland, OR (ceramicshowcase.com); ClayFest, Manitou Springs, CO (clayfest.com); and California Conference for the Advancement of Ceramics, Davis, CA (natsoulas.com/html/ccaca).

Feats of Clay, 580 6th St, Lincoln, CA. 916.645.9713. lincolnarts.org/featsofclay.htm

Artist painting by the ocean in Carmel

Driving through the Northern California flatlands full of artichoke fields to this festival, you might begin to feel like you are in a van Gogh painting. In the quaint house-lined streets of Carmel—a small town known for its galleries—75 by-invitation-only artists can be found painting *en plein air* outside in the streets, or by the beach, in the open air.

The first artist I met told us he had applied twice in the past to participate and had not been accepted. Last year he made a special weeklong trip to Carmel to paint en plein air on his own. One of the compositions he created, during that week got him a spot in this year's event. It's a very exclusive lineup of artists, for sure!

Don't think the artists have it easy painting outdoors—it can be windy, damp and cold. Being able to observe the artists create a piece is a rare and fun experience.

Each artist finishes one piece per day, and an exhibit and sale, as well as a live and silent auction, occur on Saturday night, completing the two days (Friday and Saturday) of painting. Cash prizes of $20,000 are awarded to artists in various categories. A wonderful event to attend in this idyllic town! Galleries stay open late on the Friday night of the event so you can explore.

➔ Plein air events occur all across America. Learn more about them at: thepleinairscene.com, tpaps.com, lpapa.org, borregoartinstitute.net, pleinairnewmexico.com, hawaiipleinair.com, sonomapleinair.com, outdoorpainterssociety. com, pleinairartistscolorado.com, and pleinairaustin.org.

Carmel Plein Air Festival, Dolores & 6th, Carmel, CA. 831.624.6176. carmelartfestival.org

Philadelphia on a Half-Tank by Paul Santoleri. Located at Penrose Ave & S 26th St. ©1999 City of Philadelphia Mural Arts Program. Photo by Jack Ramsdale.

The Mural Arts Program in Philadelphia is the nation's largest organization that promotes the enjoyment and production of murals. It serves nearly 2000 youth annually as well as adult offenders in local prisons and rehabilitation centers, using the restorative power of art to break the cycle of crime and violence. Since 1984, the Mural Arts Program has created over 3000 murals, earning Philadelphia international recognition as the "City of Murals." With over 50 indoor and outdoor murals created annually, all of Philadelphia's murals would stretch over 20 miles if lined up side-by-side. View wonderful examples of citywide murals at www.muralarts. org, including the Recycling Truck Project "Design In Motion," which has turned ugly dump trucks into fun-to-view vehicles. Mural Arts offers "behind the scene" tours: walking, bicycle, and trolley tours in downtown Philadelphia.

→ One of the greatest muralists of the recent past is Diego Rivera. His murals can be viewed at the Detroit Institute of Art and in San Francisco at City College of San Francisco's Diego Rivera Theatre, San Francisco Art Institute Gallery, and the City Club Stock Exchange.

→ Coit Tower in San Francisco is famous for its Depression-era murals created with WPA funds. It has a great view of the bay, too.

→ Mural towns in the U.S.: Ottawa, Il; Twenty Nine Palms, CA; Palatka, Gainesville, and Punta Gorda in FL; and Bucyrus, Massillon, Marion, and Portsmouth in OH.

→ Other mural programs across the nation:
Washington, DC: muralsdc.wordpress.com
San Francisco: precitaeyes.org
Los Angeles: sparcmurals.org; lamurals.org
St Louis: craftalliance.org/outreach/map.htm
Tucson: tucsonartsbrigade.org/murals.html
Ann Arbor: annarborchronicle.com/2010/09/16/public-art-mural-program-in-the-works
New York City: alternateroots.org/node/2038
San Antonio: sanantonio.gov/ces/murals.aspx

PHILADELPHIA'S MAGIC GARDENS

If there is one present-day artist dedicated to mosaics, it is Isaiah Zagar. When you visit his site (either online or in person), you will be able to view the awesome installations he has created throughout the neighborhood in which he lives. His heartfelt dedication to introducing the general public to beauty via his mosaic creations has worked hundredfold. More than 130 Philadelphia buildings are adorned with Zagar's mosaic murals!

Philadelphia's Magic Gardens, Zagar's largest site to date, is a folk art environment, a gallery space, and a nonprofit organization, all in one. It is a fully mosaiced indoor gallery and a staggering outdoor labyrinth of mosaic sculpture, primarily consisting of found objects. A walk through it will reveal sculptures made from bicycle wheels, handmade tiles, *objets d'art*, and mirrors of every shape and size.

Zagar has been devoted to beautifying the South Street Philadelphia neighborhood since the late 60's, when he moved to the area with

Photo ©Emily Smith

his wife Julia. The couple helped spur the revitalization of the area by purchasing and renovating derelict buildings and adding colorful mosaics on both their private and public walls. Almost solely, he has renovated this section of town and turned it into a tourist attraction. Zagar started working on Philadelphia's Magic Gardens in 1994, constructing a massive fence to protect the area. He then spent the next 14 years excavating tunnels and grottoes, sculpting multilayered walls, and tiling and grouting the 3000-square-foot space. The installation pays tribute to Zagar's many artistic influences as well as the events and experiences of his life. Tours are held on Saturday and Sunday and shouldn't be missed. For an hour and a half, you'll roam with your guide through the local streets and end up at Julia's still-thriving folk art store—The Eyes Gallery, one of Zagar's first tiling projects. Alternatively, you can take a weekend workshop from him and learn how to create your own mosaic sculptures.

His life story, *In a Dream*, produced and directed by his son, is available on video.

1020 South St, Philadelphia, PA. 215.733.0390. phillymagicgardens.org

Painting in the streets with chalk began during the Renaissance. Groups of artists called "*I Madonnari*" would follow a specific circuit from town to town to demonstrate their painting skills, providing entertainment for all. They would start painting in the evening hours and continue throughout the night. The next day, patrons would meander the streets to vote on their favorite chalkings by throwing money onto the artwork they liked best. This is how artists became known and earned a living. In recent years, chalk painting has enjoyed a renaissance. One of the best present-day events is the Italian Street Painting Festival (www.youthinarts. org) in San Rafael, California, in June—an annual two-day celebration that has thousands of visitors walking the streets to watch both professionals and children chalking their hearts out. For more street painting events: arttravelguide.info/chalk.

Melanie Stimmell van Latum

It's quite common these days to find a street painter working busily on the streets of a large city. Here, *maestra madonnara*—master street painter Melanie Stimmel van Latum—created *Special Delivery*. Melanie has won many awards around the world.
melaniestimmell.com

When you have the opportunity to attend a snow carving or ice sculpting event, you'll be able to watch the artist-teams at work, using saws, shovels, and hatchets. Happening in front of the viewing public, the sculpting becomes "performance art"—resulting in amazing creations you'll remember your entire life: slides of ice for kids to scoot down, entire buildings to walk through, huge, complex sculptures, and much more.

Snow sculpture events

→ The Saint Paul Winter Carnival in Minnesota hosts both snow and ice competitions. Over 350,000 visitors attend. It has been held since 1886, making it the oldest of its kind. winter-carnival.com

→ Since 1922, Michigan Technological University has been sponsoring an event where student-groups compete. Carving takes place throughout a month-long period; and several blocks of ice are used. Sometimes the sculpture is as tall as 28 feet and long as 125! www.mtu.edu/carnival

→ US Nationals are held during Winterfest in Lake Geneva, Wisconsin. usnationals.org

→ The International Ice Sulpture Championships in Breckenridge, Colorado, started in 1990. In January 2009, teams came all the way from China, Spain, and Holland to compete. gobreck.com

→ Illinois Snow Sculpting Competition snowsculpting.org

Ice Sculpture Events

→ World Ice Art Championships in Fairbanks, Alaska—icealaska.com—has been discontinued due to losing their land lease.

→ Private individuals proficient in ice sculpting offer their services for parties and more. icesculptureworld.com

Courtesy World Ice Art Championships

→ Zehnder's Snowfest, Frakenmuth, WI, is in its 20th year and includes both show and ice creations. zehnders.com

→ The national Ice Carving Association/ICA offers classes as well as an annual trade show and education symposium and has lists of ice carvers in your area. nica.org

→ Ice carving has become popular with high-end restaurants for centerpieces for buffets. academyoficecarving.com

For more snow and ice sculpture events: arttravelguide.info/ice

Sand Sculpture Competition, Cannon Beach, OR

It was amazing to discover sand sculpture events and the extent to which artists have taken their sculpting skills with this medium, producing huge sand sculptures, some even large enough to drive cars through!

Artists who are into sand sculpting have many opportunities to win monetary awards—up to $10,000—through competitions held worldwide in China, Netherlands, Denmark, Canada, and the US. Most competitions have pro and novice divisions. In the pro division, one artist usually designs the piece and has assistants help build it. Sometimes, sand is put into forms and soaked with water in order to prepare the medium that will yield the art. These transitory competitions usually take place on a beach. When the tide comes in, the elusive sculpture disappears, and photographs are the only memory.

Bluebeard's Castle, constructed in 1985 at Treasure Island, Florida, was the world-record breaker for size—a football-field long and 37 feet high. It was equipped with access roads, enabling thousands of people to tour the sand city.

Todd Vander Pluym, president of Sand Sculptors International (sandsculptors.com), has sculpted 1500 sculptures around the globe from South Africa to Japan. He has won nearly 200 sand sculpting titles, including four world championships. Trained as an architect, he and his employees create sculptures at malls and events and for corporations. *Sleeping Beauty's Castle* in Santa Monica was the indoor recordbreaker in 1987: 20 feet high with 170 tons of sand.

For more sand events: arttravelguide.info/sand

The McMenamin brothers are well known in the Pacific Northwest for saving and renovating about-to-be demolished schools and buildings. Edgefield is one of their many accomplishments.

My mother, who grew up in a neighboring town in the 20's, remembers her father talking about the Poor Farm when she was young. He would tease the kids, "If you don't work hard, you'll end up at the Poor Farm." It sounded bad, so they worked hard. Years later (75), I took her to see the Poor Farm—now Edgefield and a wonderful retreat. The Poor Farm was built in 1911 by liberal social-welfare thinkers. It had a population in 1935 of 614 (535 men). During the Depression, the farm peaked in population. In the 60's it was made into a nursing home. By the 80's, the fight to save it began with the help of the Troutdale Historical Society. By 1990, it was named to the National Register of Historic Places and was purchased by the McMenamin brothers.

As usual, it was a masterful rennovation job. The walls, nooks, doors, and overhead pipes all boast extraordinary artwork by a team of living artists. What were once classrooms have been converted into hotel rooms—over 100. A small community of buildings makes up the large compound, once used to farm food and pleasant now to stroll through. The Distillery Bar made me feel like I had been transported to a small town in Ireland; the hobbit-sized Little Red Shed—my favorite spot to relax—comfortably seats 10 people. Ivy-covered and cozy, it once served as an incinerator for the property.

You will encounter surprise after surprise as you stroll through the colorful grounds only 20 minutes from Portland.

2126 SW Halsey St, Troutdale, OR. 503.669.8610. mcmenamins.com

Cracking Art, Red Penguin, 2005. Plastic. Monica Mahoney, *Arillated: The 21c Pip Mobile,* 2005-2007. Glass gems, silicone, 1995 Lincoln Towne Car stretch limousine. Photo by Kenneth Hayden, 2008. Courtesy of 21c Museum Hotel.

21c Museum Hotel was founded in 2006 by Laura Lee Brown and Steve Wilson, philanthropists and arts patrons who had a vision: supporting the revitalization of Louisville's downtown and engaging the public with contemporary art in a new way. Understanding that art drives commerce and enriches people's lives, they created 21c Museum Hotel to help make Louisville and its historic downtown arts and theater district a more vibrant place.

The hotel has 90 rooms featuring 9000 square feet. Visitors not staying at the hotel can also view the contemporary art museum, a stunning collection of cutting-edge art. Group and solo exhibitions feature emerging artists alongside acclaimed international artists—Bill Viola, Tony Oursler, Andres Serrano, Sam Taylor Wood, David Leventhal, Yinka Shonibare and Judy Fox, Chuck Close, Alfredo Jaar, and Kara Walker. Exhibits are displayed in elevators, public restrooms, sunken courtyards, hallways, on the walls of the Proof on Main restaurant and bar—even on the floor!

21c is a critical and financial success and has proven once again that art venues attract tourists. (Bilboa might be the best example!) The 21c team is looking towards opportunities to enliven the cultural and civic life in urban centers across the country, including Bentonville, Arkansas and Cincinnati, Ohio.

700 W Main St, Louisville, KY. 502.217.6300. 21cmuseumhotel.com

You can now experience an overnight stay in a house designed by Frank Lloyd Wright; rent one of the facilities listed below.

Louis Penfield House
A two-story spruce and concrete-block house with unusually high doorways for the unusually tall proprietor; custom furniture.
Willoughby, OH. penfieldhouse.com

John D Haynes House
Made of brick and red-tidewater cypress, this house cost twice what the owner originally requested. It is highlighted by a dramatic cantilevered fireplace.
Fort Wayne, IN. hayneshousellc.com

Bernard Schwartz House
A four-bedroom house built of brick and red-tidewater cypress; three fireplaces (one outdoor), and a zig-zagging second-floor interior balcony overlooking the 65-foot-long living room. Stunning.
Two Rivers, WI. theschwartzhouse.com

Seth Peterson Cottage
This one-bedroom retreat features a dramatic slanted roof with expansive windows revealing the forest and lake. A canoe is provided to explore the lake.
Lake Delton, WI. sethpeterson.org

Duncan House
This prefabricated house was rescued from demolition near Chicago and reconstructed an hour's drive east of Pittsburgh. The concrete block fireplace was rebuilt in stone during renovation, an upgrade option Wright specified in his original plans. Original ceramic tiles still grace one bathroom.
Laurel Highlands, PA. polymathpark.com

Inn at the Price Tower
Built in 1956 for an oil pipeline company, this slender glass-sheathed building is the only skyscraper actually built that was designed by Wright. It is now a National Historical Landmark. Tours are available of the tower. The building currently houses Price Tower Arts Center. The art center is beginning to collect dynamic contemporary art: Robert Indiana's monumental sculpture *Sixty-Six* (2004) and numerous pieces by Dennis Oppenheim. The museum hosts three exhibitions annually.

Also within the National Historical Landmark is a 19-room boutique hotel—Inn at The Price Tower. I M Pei's disciple Wendy Evans Joseph designed the guest rooms with Japanese style textiles, Tibetan wool carpets, and wood and copper tubing.

A restaurant, The Copper Bar, on the 15th floor offers spectacular views and was inspired by Wright's Prairie School design.

510 Dewey Ave, Bartlesville, OK. 918.336.4949. pricetower.org

Courtesy of Price Tower Arts Center

House of Blues, San Diego. Courtesy House of Blues.

This chain of clubs (houseofblues.com) is a favorite of mine; I try to go to them in any city I might visit. Art is everywhere—walls, ceiling, hallways, bathrooms—mostly folk art. Live music is most common too. Often, both lunch and dinner are served.

The San Diego club has a Bead Wall—an entire wall covered in Mardi Gras beads.

The Las Vegas club has over 300 pieces of original folk art and 50,000 bottle caps incorporated into Mr Imagination's mural decorating the entrance.

The Chicago club is modeled after the spectacular "Estavovski" Opera House in Prague.

Anaheim is home to the unique Quilts of Gees Bend. Some of the pieces displayed date back to the early 1900's and have been featured on US postage stamps.

Cleveland has been retrofitted into an old Woolworth's department store building and spans 61,000 square feet.

You'll find more wonders in New Orleans, Dallas, Houston, Atlantic City, Boston, Los Angeles, Myrtle Beach, and Orlando.

Art sites are listed in bold type; titles of books, magazines, artworks, and videos are in italic type.